CARTOON COOK BOOK

... for men

by
Ron Page

authorHOUSE

AuthorHouse™ UK Ltd.
500 Avebury Boulevard
Central Milton Keynes, MK9 2BE
www.authorhouse.co.uk
Phone: 08001974150

© 2007 Ron Page. All rights reserved.

No part of this book may be reproduced, stored in a retrieval system, or transmitted by any means without the written permission of the author.

First published by AuthorHouse 8/30/2007

ISBN: 978-1-4343-2398-9 (sc)

Printed in the United States of America
Bloomington, Indiana

This book is printed on acid-free paper.

The author would like to record that he has had no formal training in cookery and has written this book on the basis of his own knowledge and experience.

THANKS TO

It should be noted that no animals have been used to test the recipes in this book although it must be admitted that my daughter's dog Sally has occasionally snaffled leftovers and has survived without ill effects. Rather I must thank my family and friends for volunteering to undergo the testing process from which, I am pleased to say, they emerged more often than not with smiles on their faces, licking their lips and asking for more. I would particularly like to thank Mr. Leon Balen and Mr. Damian Davies for the illustrations and the interest shown in the book.

LAUGHS ON THE WAY TO THE KITCHEN

"One in four men would post their loved one a cook book rather than the Kama Sutra according to a Royal Mail survey. It found that only 16% would send a sex manual."
Daily Mail 1997

"(England) is the only country in the world where food is more dangerous than sex."
Jackie Mason

"I like children but I could not eat a whole one."
W.C.Fields

On being asked why he never drank water - "Fish mate in it"
W.C.Fields (sanitized)

"Can I have a table nearer the floor? Certainly I'll have the waiter cut the legs off."
Groucho Marx

"A cucumber should be well sliced and dressed with pepper and vinegar then thrown out as good for nothing."
Samuel Johnson

"What I always say about your salads Annie is that I may not enjoy eating them but I learn an awful lot about insect biology."
Alan Ayckbourn

"An invitation to come in for a cup of coffee has a different meaning today. In my day all you got was coffee."
Sad Old Man

"When I am invited in for a cup of coffee all I want is coffee."
Sadder Older Man

THE MENU

Chapter		Page
1	What !! Me Cook ??? - why bother ?	7
2	Getting Converted - to metric and imperial.	15
3	Keeping it Clean - in the kitchen.	16
4	Speaking the Language - of cooking.	18
5	Teasing the Palate - with fruit, soups, pâtés, and other nice things.	22
6	Satisfaction - In the Main ? - with chicken, beef, lamb and ham.	53
7	For Full Satisfaction - eat vegetables, rice and pasta.	88
8	Honeymoon and other Salads - with dressings.	95
9	If You Must - make pastry.	98
10	Sweet Things - getting your just "desserts".	101
11	If I Knew You Were Coming - I would have baked a cake.	136
12	Cheese and Wine - what a nice way to finish.	151

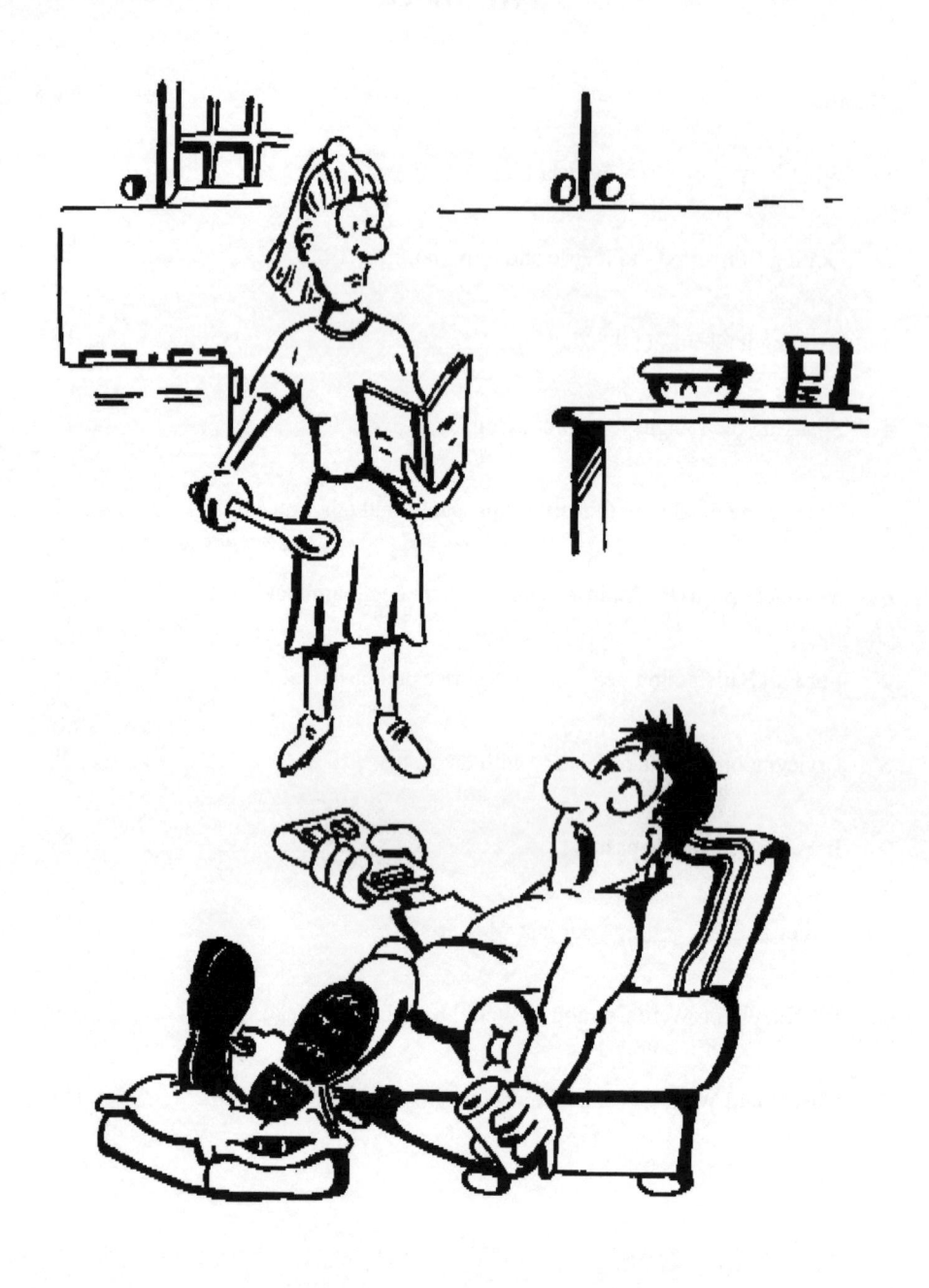

What! Me cook?

WHAT !! ME COOK ???

Sex and sport are the subjects of main interest to the average man with food coming a close third. However, whereas most men will read extensively about sex and sport to improve their knowledge and performance their interest in food rarely extends beyond the dinner table. The aim of this book is to stimulate an interest in cooking and to teach those who become interested how to cook a variety of dishes which will please their palate and impress their partners. However, it is not about basic cooking such as how to boil an egg, make gravy or cook the typical British Sunday roast, but it does provide simple well-tried recipes which will enable you to cook to a standard which will surprise you.

The title of this book was chosen because I hope it will appeal to men (and perhaps women) who are keen to learn how to cook high quality meals in a simple way using ingredients readily available often from cans. At one time an interest in cooking was thought to be effeminate as the division of labour demanded that men made money and women stayed at home with their children and cooked the meals. Now when roles are being reversed an ability to cook is recognised as another aspect of a well balanced man, capable of looking after himself in all situations. However there is still much room for improvement. A 1994 survey of 2,000 men and women of all ages for the Office of Population, Censuses and Surveys found that the majority of both sexes thought it important for boys as well as girls to be taught to cook. Despite this, eighty per cent of women prepared every meal put on the table at home, even jobless men were reluctant to take over the cooking and not surprisingly older men were less likely to be found in the kitchen. So even today the image of the caring sharing man is not quite a reality.

A little history will explain how the book came to be written. After we were married, my wife and I, like most young couples were invited by friends to their homes for dinner, but it soon became apparent that my wife, who is an excellent British style cook, was unhappy at her inability to reciprocate the curries, lasagnes and satays with which we were being entertained. Although thinking it would be just a passing interest some years later I attended an Indian cookery class at night school, and finding enjoyment in the cooking as well as the eating, began to collect the recipes which are contained in this book. Where have they come from? Many of them have been given to me by friends in different parts of the world, but it must be said that most come from conventional sources such as other cookery books, magazines and newspapers. However for every recipe selected at least ten have been tried and rejected - either they were complicated, involved rare and exotic ingredients, took much too long to prepare or just did not work. Consequently you will not find in this book recipes such as "Lobster with garlic aioli", nor will you be required to slave for hours over a hot stove using ingredients which you have obtained only after much difficulty.

In my search for information some cookery books with myriads of pretty pictures looked nice but caused much frustration in that recipes just did not work. The view of one well known cookery expert that Fanny Craddock, an early television chef, was a marvellous entertainer "but in all my years I have never found one of her recipes that actually worked" is one with which I have much sympathy. Also television cookery programmes were often more entertaining than instructional and I wondered at times whether the star chef was having fun at my expensive. Did one such star on a tour of Tuscany really expect me to be able to buy bull's blood and testicles at my local supermarket so that I could emulate his culinary masterpiece?

The number of recipes which became recipes for disaster and the number of times the results of my efforts had to be thrown in the waste bin was astonishing. Later in the book you will find a recipe for ice cream which produces a superb end-product but since it contains a lot of cream I tried as a more healthy alternative a recipe based on evaporated milk. One of the stages involved placing the ice cream in a freezer and after a set period stirring to break up the crystals which had formed. Have you ever tried stirring a solid block of ice? To make matters worse the chips of ice I tried tasted ugh!

Because of the intrinsic attraction of a recipe - it may have an unusual combination of ingredients or provide a simple way of making a dish - I have often persisted and made a number of attempts to get it right. When successful these recipes have been included. Some recipes I reject out of hand. One much vaunted chef in a magazine article described how to make the toffee for a toffee and banana crumble as follows - "place a tin of condensed milk in a pan of water, boil for three hours topping up with boiling water as necessary". Is the man mad I thought - does he really expect me to hang around in a kitchen for three hours to make a dessert which will be scoffed in less than five minutes? I enjoy cooking but draw the line at drudgery.

Why follow my example and learn to cook? Firstly, wives and girl friends cannot fail to be impressed that you have slaved over a hot stove to please them - with most of the recipes in this book this does not really apply as the majority have been selected for their speed and ease of preparation - and perhaps the old saying that the way to a man's heart is through his stomach can be augmented by the thought that maybe the way to a woman's bedroom is via your kitchen. Having said this, do not be tempted to dabble with foods that have the reputation of heightening desire. Over the years aphrodisiac properties have been ascribed to almost every fruit, vegetable and flower. Some foods seem to be linked to sexual desire by their resemblance to human genitalia - bananas, carrots and asparagus can mimic the erect penis while oysters and mussels have been likened to the vulva. The interest in rhinohorn in some countries is probably similarly explained. No - the chemistry you should aim for to spark a relationship is that produced by eating a good meal with good wine in a pleasant relaxed atmosphere.

Secondly eating out at restaurants is often expensive and not good value for money - you pay a lot for poor quality meals. This is particularly true at Christmas when the maximum number of people are squeezed into every available space and you sit so close that you are never quite sure whether you are eating from your plate or your neighbour's!! This is the time when prepacked and precooked turkey is heated in a microwave and served "with all the trimmings in the best tradition of Christmas fare", to be followed by an ultra sweet concoction described as Black Forest Gateau. At any time of the year it is difficult to get good food at reasonable prices in the U.K. and this problem is compounded by food critics who after dining at restaurants free, recommend

Cartoon Cook Book… for Men

them to their readers who can pay almost the equivalent of a day's pay for a meal for two.

It is difficult to understand why eating out in countries such as France and America is so much better value for money than in this country - meals are usually both better and cheaper. Good food is important to the French who treat meals as occasions to be lingered over as one of life's great pleasures. You would therefore expect dining out to be more expensive but as you drive through France, wherever you stop you will find small cafes providing quality meals at reasonable prices. Even in America where the standard of living is so much higher than in the U.K. eating out as distinct from dining out provides much more for your money.

Eating out on a budget in the United Kingdom is usually limited to fish and chips, burgers, pizzas, the British cooked breakfast on offer in cafes before 11am and pub food all of which have their devotees. Fish and chips freshly cooked can be delicious, and the same is true of the British breakfast which offers a lot of calories for the money. Burger and pizza bars generally serve food which is tasteless but has the advantage that it is cheap, will not harm you and has popular appeal especially for children. A friend who is fond of good food told me that one of the most welcome sights on holiday in Japan was turning a corner to find an international chain burger bar. His burger meal came as a welcome change after two weeks of rice, sushi and teriyaki, and was guaranteed not to make him ill or break the bank. For these reasons and their convenience, fast food chains are spreading even in France although it came as a surprise to find a burger bar in the Champs-Elysées in Paris only 100 metres from the Arc de Triumphe.

If asked to advise visitors from abroad who wish to count their pennies when eating out in the U.K. I would recommend pub food which although unenterprising is usually good, wholesome and reasonably priced - some of the pubs with national chain restaurants are surprisingly good. A number of years ago Indian restaurants could be guaranteed to provide delicious meals at low cost - indeed one of my favourite dining experiences was in a cafe in Bradford where we sat at formica topped tables and dipped our chapptis in the curry as no cutlery was provided. Now however many Indian restaurants have refurbished and gone up market by charging for a main course what one can pay for a three course meal in many Paris bistros. To add insult to injury a comprehensive wine list is usually offered with prices only a madman would pay - how can one appreciate wine with a spicy curry which if anything overwhelms the taste buds - cold beer or water is a much better bet.

At one time I was fortunate to be employed to entertain guests from abroad and was paid to dine at some of the best restaurants in the country. I am sorry to say that more often than not I was disappointed to find the food pretentious and looking pretty at the expense of taste. Dining out at a fancy restaurant can be a disaster for the average man who can be intimidated by a menu in French and waiters who give the impression that they are doing their customers a favour by allowing them to eat at their establishment. Some chefs have been known to refuse to serve a steak well done in the arrogant belief that they know best. If you find yourself in these circumstances, be pleasant but firm and get what you asked for.

Cartoon Cook Book… for Men

Sometimes, but in my view not often, eating out at what at first sight seems an exorbitant cost can be good value for money if it provides an experience which is exceptional in terms of the quality of the food or the splendour of the surroundings. Experiences which I treasure are of dining at a restaurant at the top of the highest building in San Francisco from which the views over the bay were dazzling and spending a weekend in a French chateau where the food was simply superb. However, eating out can be exciting and even sensual without being expensive. At the age of eighteen when cycling through France, some friends and I sat in the middle of a field on a very dark night eating bread and cheese washed down with an oversupply of cheap red wine. The memory of that night always makes me smile.

Many self styled judges of good food say that British food is stodgy and unimaginitive but for me the traditional Sunday lunch of a roast with a variety of vegetables and lashings of gravy as prepared by the average British housewife takes some beating. Unfortunately the same meal outside the home is not easily available - even in a pub on Sunday or a carvery the food looks the same but never quite comes up to the same standard. Nevertheless as I have said before pubs give good value for money and as a result sale of food in pubs is booming and in some, account for 50% of their takings.

Coming now to the question of healthy eating, everybody knows that a diet high in fibre and low in fat makes for a healthier life. This does not mean however that we have to cut out all our favourite foods and live on lettuce and tomatoes as a well balanced diet can embrace all types of foods provided that we practise moderation. A diet guru once on radio proclaimed that the smell of fish and chips made his mouth water but he resisted temptation and walked past the shop with an air of self-righteousness. What nonsense - something we like whether it be fish and chips or a burger if taken occasionally will not drag us down the path to ill-health and obesity. Do not be misled however by the eat what you like brigade - diet is important and allergies to food are real and not imaginary. About 2% of adults are thought to be affected by unpleasant reactions to certain foods such as milk, eggs, cheese, peanuts, wheat, fish and particularly shellfish. Allergic reactions can involve itching, rashes, headaches and breathing difficulties. A personal example is that of my wife who on holiday some years ago in Cyprus reacted so violently to a meal that she was unable to walk more than a few yards and had to be rushed to hospital for treatment. She had experienced an asthma attack which she still suffers from even to this day, although prior to the holiday she had never shown any symptoms of the disease. The culprit was thought to be the shellfish she consumed as part of a Greek meze which has been noted elsewhere for triggering asthma. Since then my wife has religiously avoided shellfish except on one occasion when she was tempted to try one mussel from my plate when on holiday in Spain. The reaction was so unpleasant she swears never again!! One modern trend is to move away from meat and become vegetarian in a quest for a healthy diet. If you do not like meat your decision to abstain is understandable but those who refuse to eat meat on moral or quasi religious grounds should understand that this is contrary to nature in that your body has been designed to digest meat as well as vegative products. Human beings are omnivorous as nature or God, if you believe in God, has intended.

Now we come to my golden rules of cooking-

1. Cook only meals that you yourself enjoy - do not be tempted to try something which is not quite to your taste just to please friends because you will not enjoy the end-product and in addition it will be difficult to judge whether the quality is up to standard. You must of course be aware of your guest's likes and dislikes especially if they have food allergies or special dietary needs. Cater for their tastes by all means as it would be foolish to serve something they did not like, but make sure the dish is one you all enjoy.

2. Enjoy your cooking - if you do not enjoy cooking do not bother. Why slave over a hot stove if you do not enjoy it when you can buy something ready prepared be it a sauce or complete meal which is often just as acceptable. One of the first things I learnt about cooking is why convenience foods are so popular. Good cooking can be very time consuming and a man living alone coming home tired from work or a young mother with children cannot always spare the time to put quality food on the table. However the purpose of this book is to show you easy ways of producing quality dishes at a fraction of the cost you would pay in a restaurant or take-away.

3. Make it easy on yourself - if you have invited friends for dinner organise well ahead and never plan a multi course meal which involves much cooking on the night - precook as much as you can so all you need do is take dishes from the freezer and reheat to serve. If your meal imposes on you and your guests a strict timetable for example you have to finish your starter by 8 o'clock so that the main course will not be overdone, think again. If your main course is ambitious, serve a simple starter and dessert which can be prepared well ahead of time.

4. Never experiment on guests - if you see a recipe you like, try it out on yourself before serving it to friends. Hopefully the recipes in this book should be achieveable at the first time of trying, but if things go wrong and you are attracted by the dish keep on trying until you are happy with the end result. Never cook for guests a dish that you are not completely sure of.

5. If necessary cheat - if you have invited friends to a meal and things start going wrong or you become short of time do not hesitate to substitute what you have planned with starters, desserts, and even main courses which you have bought previously and stored in your freezer. Whether you claim the meal as all your own work is a matter for you, but why not?

6. Cook with dash - while there is no need to emulate the antics of the more flamboyant television cooks by cooking with a glass of wine in your hand, do not be afraid to cut a dash in your own kitchen. While it is foolish to experiment when you have a special dinner party there is nothing to stop you being bold in terms of recipes or presentation when cooking for yourself or a close friend. For example although you should try to follow the recipes as closely as possible, remember you are not making up a doctor's prescription so do not be overconcerned to measure out the ingredients precisely. If you think you would like more of one ingredient by all means please yourself. With some ingredients you must be careful - there is a marked difference in taste between half and one teaspoon of chilli powder!

7. Be kind to your guests - do not pile up their plates with the implied threat that if they do not scrape them clean it will be seen as an insult to your cooking. Let them help themselves to as little or as much as they like. By all means, encourage them to have seconds because some people are slow in coming forward, but remember we all have our likes and dislikes. To be forced by politeness to wade through a mountain of food which one does not like is enough to scar one for life. This happened to me! When I was a small boy an aunt gave me seedcake to which I took an instant dislike. Surrounded by my father, aunt and other relatives I remember to this day how sick I felt as every mouthful was forced down.

Coming now to the question of presentation, the difference between eating out at the local cafe and a good restaurant is not just the quality of the food but also the presentation. An attractively laid table in a relaxingly lit setting is all important. There are basic rules about laying the table, setting out the cutlery, flower arrangements and there is also the art of cutting vegetables in the form of flutes, stars etc. which can make food even more attractive. Neither subject is covered here. Apart from an interest in seductive lighting to create an ambiance of relaxation and comfort, I usually leave presentation to my wife. This does not help the reader so perhaps I could suggest that most girls would be flattered by an invitation to dinner on the understanding that you will slave over a hot stove in exchange for some assistance with laying the table (and washing up?).

If you live alone you may be inclined to survive on precooked meals, sitting in a chair watching television which is understandable after a hard day but remember that inviting friends to dinner perhaps at the weekend gives you the opportunity of demonstrating your cooking skills and helps to redress the culinary imbalance.

In writing this book I have assumed that you have basic equipment available - in addition you will benefit by the use of a freezer, electric blender, whisk and coffee grinder, the latter being used to grind spices. Hopefully by now you will have realised that this is not a glossy fantasy cookbook which you buy to put on a shelf to impress your friends but a down-to-earth collection of clear and simple recipes with perhaps a touch of sophistication. Good food, good wine and good company - what a lovely way to spend an evening. Let me wish that this book helps you enjoy many such occasions.

Finally if you get around to reading this book but never get around to trying any of the recipes perhaps I could leave you with this one thought. If friends are kind enough to invite you into their home to wine and dine, be thankful for the compliment, and never ever go away criticising the standard of the food served or indeed any other aspect of what has been provided for your enjoyment. If you are not happy, keep it to yourself and politely decline the next time you are invited.

Cartoon Cook Book... for Men

GETTING CONVERTED

These tables enable you to convert metric to imperial measures and vice versa. They are approximate conversions which have been rounded up or down. For example 4 ounces is about 113 grams - in the table the equivalent is given as 110 grams. Remember always use either metric or imperial measures - never mix the two.

Oven Temperatures

Mark	°F	°C
1	275	140
2	300	150
3	325	170
4	350	180
5	375	190
6	400	200
7	425	220
8	450	230

Weights

ounce	gram
½	10
1	25
1½	40
2	50
2½	60
3	75
4	110
5	150
6	175
7	200
8	225
9	250
10	275
12	350
1lb	450
1½lb	700
2lb	900

Lengths

inch	cm
½	1
1	2.5
1½	4
2	5
3	7.5
4	10
5	13
6	15
7	18
8	20
9	23
10	25.5
11	28
12	30

Volumes

pint	ml
¼	150
½	300
1	600
1¾	1 litre

Abbreviations

F = degrees Fahrenheit
oz = ounce
lb = pound
floz = fluid ounce
Note 20 floz = one pint
tbsp = tablespoon
Mark = refers to gas ovens

C = degrees Centigrade
g = gram (also gramme)
cm = centimetre
ml = millilitre
l = litre
tsp = teaspoon

KEEPING IT CLEAN

Keeping your kitchen clean is of paramount importance, yet very few cookery books deal with cleanliness and hygiene. Anyone interested in cooking should be aware that many foods contain harmful bacteria which have the potential to cause food poisoning and in addition the kitchen is the part of the home where accidents are most likely to occur.

It goes without saying that when dealing with food your hands, equipment and working surfaces should be spotlessly clean but there are some essential points which need stressing here -

1. Any food that smells or even looks not quite right should be discarded no matter what the cost. It is better to be safe than sorry as your guests will not thank you if they wake up the next morning with upset stomachs.

2. Heat kills bacteria so make sure that food is cooked right through and that poultry from the freezer is completely defrosted before cooking.

3. Wash your hands before and after handling meat and poultry and when uncooked do not let them come in contact with other foods. Do not use the same knives or utensils for raw and uncooked foods without washing them in between.

4. Never refreeze food taken from the freezer. Keep some ice cubes in a cup in your freezer so that you can recognise immediately if there has been a power cut or failure of the freezer by the cubes melting to one level. If this happens you will need to think about the safety of the food even though it has become rock solid again following the power return.

5. Do not put hot food in the refrigerator as this will warm up the air and may allow bacteria to thrive. Cool first.

Remember that all human activities have some dangers associated with them and this is true of cooking. A few years ago concern about salmonella in eggs engrossed the public interest as newspapers reported at length the furore between farmers and politicians about the risks involved. Although no one can guarantee that the eggs you buy today are salmonella free, the subject has gone out of fashion and the general public seems no longer interested. What you should know is that from almost time immemorial chefs have used uncooked eggs to prepare certain dishes believing the risks to be very small and worth taking. Using uncooked eggs is like driving a car - there is a risk but it is for you decide whether or not it is acceptable.

Strict standards of hygiene in dealing with all foods will ensure that the risks are minimal. Be especially vigilant in making sure that you and your guests suffer no harm in the kitchen from dangers such as boiling liquids, hot dishes and sharp knives.

Cartoon Cook Book… for Men

SPEAKING THE LANGUAGE

In March 1994 I spent a week at a four star hotel in Cornwall which had a reputation for good food. The meals were of a high standard and I was pleased that each course was served at the table so that I could enjoy my meal at leisure. You may think that this was as it should be but more and more hotels are introducing buffets as a means of reducing costs - the word "buffet" sums up it up in my view as one is buffeted and jostled among the crowd striving to serve oneself.

To be fair, the hotel had a lot to offer but there were some things I did not like. The chef was a devotee of nouvelle cuisine and emphasised the appearance and presentation of each dish to the extent that the food gave the impression of being painted on to the plates. The desserts were particularly colourful, no doubt the effect of food dyes, but were the pretty patterns more inviting to the hotel guests than the natural colours and smell of a hearty British style pudding such as apple pie and cream? It is to be deplored that chefs are now thinking of themselves as food artists and designers rather than cooks. Decor and presentation are important but much less so than the quality of the food as defined by its freshness, depth of taste, texture and colour.

Being in a Cornish hotel I also wondered what had happened to Cornish cuisine and where was the Cornish pasty for which the area is famous. To make matters worse the menu described its offerings with words such as ganache, bavarois, paupiette, and millefieulle. I doubted whether one percent of the hotel's guests knew the meaning of every word on the menu - I certainly did not. This is not surprising since some of these words cannot be found in English or even some French dictionaries. What did the hotel gain by using such words - were its guests impressed or just confused? The purpose of a menu is to tell you what you can order not to promote conversation between waiters and guests who have to ask what the words mean. I prefer to be impressed by the quality of the food not by the chef's command of another tongue but as long as restaurants delight in using these words you will be at a disadvantage if you do not learn to speak the language. For this reason I have somewhat reluctantly included the following list of words to know.

Ail	garlic
A la	in the style of
A la carte	dishes priced separately
Alfresco	in the open air
Al dente	pasta still firm to the bite
Bain-marie	water bath for slow heating
Bavarois	a light custard usually set with gelatine
Bouillon	thin soup or broth
Bouquet garni	a bundle of herbs used for flavouring

Broil	American term for grilling
Canapé	a small piece of bread or pastry with a savoury on top
Chateaubriand	a thick fillet of beef steak
Cocotte	a small fireproof dish for cooking and serving an individual portion of food
Coulis	thick purée of of fruit or vegetables
Crêpes	thin pancakes
Devilled	highly seasoned with hot flavouring
Egg wash	beaten egg brushed on to food to facilitate browning during cooking
Escargot	edible snail
Frappé	served chilled or with crushed ice
Fricassee	stewed pieces of meat served in a thick white sauce
Fume	smoked
Galantine	white meat or fish served cold in aspic
Galette	a small flat cake of potato, vegetables etc.
Ganache	chocolate and cream
Glace	ice cream
Goujon	fish strips deep fried in egg and crumbs
Jardinière	a dish of vegetables cut in thin strips
Grenouilles	frogs
Macédoine	vegetables or fruit cut up small
Macerate / **Marinade**	make soft by steeping in wine, vinegar, oil, spices etc. before cooking - macerate usually applies to fruit whereas marinade relates to meat
Medaillon	round shaped portion of meat or fish
Millefeiulle	puff pastry filled with jam and cream
Mousse	light sweet or savoury dish
Navarin	lamb stew
Noisette d'Agneau	a cut of lamb
Parfait	a specialty ice cream
Paupiette	slices of meat stuffed and rolled up
Paysanne	country or peasant style
Plat du jour	dish of the day
Prosciutto	Italian Parma ham
Provencale	regional or provincial style
Rennet	curdling agent obtained from a calf stomach used to make cheese

Rondeau	round shallow cooking vessel
Sauté	shallow fried
Sec	dry as applied to wine
Soufflé	a light sweet or savoury made with beaten egg whites
Spatchcock	chicken spread-eagled for cooking
Table d'hôte	menu at a set price
Timbale	drum shaped serving vessel
Tournedos	a small round thick cut from a fillet of beef
Truffle	an edible fungus
Vin blanc	white wine
Vin rouge	red wine
Zabaglione	a light Italian sweet
Zest	orange or lemon peel used as flavouring

Cartoon Cook Book… for Men

TEASING - THE PALATE !!

First courses are designed to tease the palate and stimulate interest in what is to come so they should be light and tasty. Also they should be easy to prepare leaving you relaxed and able to enjoy your own meal. There are no rules about what can be served to begin a meal and starters can vary from soup, salads, and pasta to small portions of more substantial dishes - generally light dishes which whet the appetite, leaving your guests in the mood to do justice to the main course are preferred.

Food will only be appetising if it is attractive to look at. Colour and texture are very important and a meal which consists mainly of dishes which are white or bland in colour will not please the eye. Aim for a good balance of colour, texture and richness so after deciding on your main course select a starter to complement it. If your guests scrape their plates and are hungry for the main course you can lick your own lips with the satisfaction that you got it right.

Finally note that any of the starters can form the basis of a light lunch or high tea as a change from sandwiches or something on toast - admittedly they do take a little more time to prepare.

Baked Potato

MENU - STARTERS

Fruit   **Page**

1. Hot Ginger Grapefruit. 24
2. Avocado Salad. 25
3. Melon and Ginger with Port. 25

Soups

1. Melon and Mint. 26
2. Stilton and Celery. 28
3. French Onion. 29
4. Carrot. 30
5. Curried Parsnip. 31
6. Mint Pea. 32

Pâtés

1. Salmon and Lemon. 33
2. Taramasalata. 35
3. Guacamole. 36

Other Nice Things

1. Stuffed Aubergines. 37
2. Leeks and Ham with Cheese Sauce. 38
3. Chicken Lemons. 39
4. Leek Soufflé. 40
5. Roasted Peppers. 43
6. Glamorgan Sausages. 44
7. Deep Fried Camembert. 45
8. Garlic Mushrooms. 46
9. Kipper Fish Cakes. 47
10. Sardine Triangles. 48
11. Smoked Salmon and Scrambled Eggs. 49
12. Onion Bhaji. 50
13. Yorkshire Pudding and Curry Sauce. 51

Hot Ginger Grapefruit

This is a light starter which is ideal before a substantial main course. There is a point worth making here. Remember that people's tastes vary so always check if you can that what you plan to serve will be welcomed by your guests - for example not everyone likes the sharpness of grapefruit. I once had the embarrassment of watching a friend picking bits of vegetable out of a dish I had served while insisting that although he did not like the vegetable he loved the rest of it. This is like saying you enjoyed the meal but were grateful for a small appetite!

metric	*Ingredients*	*imperial*
2	grapefruits	2
4tbsp	sherry	4tbsp
2tbsp	brown sugar	2tbsp
1tsp	ground ginger	1tsp

Method

Cut the grapefruits in half which gives one each for four people. Mix the other ingredients together and stir well. Since ground ginger does not wet down easily warm slightly by placing the mixture in a microwave for about 30 seconds. Pour the mixture over the grapefruit halves then grill or microwave until hot.

Notes

It is a good idea to put sugar on the table so that your guests can help themselves if the grapefruits are too sharp. Some, such as Florida grapefruits, are sweeter than others so the amount of sugar used in the recipe will usually require a little thought. Use white sugar if brown is not available.

Avocado Salad

You will see a lot of nonsense written about salads such as - they cleanse and invigorate the system and by eating them you will be giving yourself a beauty treatment. All I would say is that they can be very tasty and are good for you so you can only benefit if you use them in your diet for example as a substantial part of a main course or as a light starter.

To serve four people, for this starter you will need 2 ripe avocados, 2tbsp lemon juice, 1 tbsp olive oil, ½ tsp sugar, half a small onion, 4 tomatoes, a pinch each of salt and pepper, and some lettuce and cucumber the amount depending on how much you like in a salad. Making the salad is very simple - cut each avocado in half, remove the stone and scoop out the flesh in small chunks with a spoon and place in a bowl, grate in the onion, cut up the tomatoes, cucumber and lettuce, add them to the bowl and mix thoroughly together. Now put the lemon juice, olive oil, salt, pepper and sugar in a bowl and whisk with a fork. Pour the dressing over the salad and it is ready to eat. There is one aspect of salads worth mentioning here - there is quite an art in cutting and shaping fruit and vegetables to make them look attractive, for example tomatoes can be cut with scalloped edges and cucumber can be cut into whirls with a potato peeler. While I think a lot of embellishment is completely unnecessary shaping vegetables is an art worth giving some thought to.

Melon and Ginger with Port

This a very simple light starter which requires no cooking. For four people you need one melon, four tablespoons of port and one of crystallised ginger. Simply cut the melon in four, remove the pips and with a sharp knife slice the flesh away from the rind, then cut along and across so as to leave the chunks in position on the rind. Pour a tablespoon of port on each piece of melon and sprinkle on the ginger finely chopped. You can leave out the ginger and use sherry or any spirit accordingly to taste and availability.

Melon and Mint Soup

Perhaps because I have been brought up to think of soups as winter warmers on a cold day I have never been partial to soups designed to be eaten cold. One such soup, gazpacho made from oil, garlic and onions is very popular in Spain but when on holiday there I have rarely ordered it. One exception to my aversion to cold soups is made from the recipe which follows as it is both delicious and different. Served on a hot day perhaps when sitting in a garden it is particularly refreshing but it goes down well any time as a light starter before a substantial main course.

For four people you will need 2 melons, 2tbsp lemon juice, 4tbsp mint jelly and 4tsp of sugar. For decorative purposes halve each melon by making even zig zag cuts around the circumference about an inch long - when they join cut deeper so that the melons separate. Discard the seeds and scoop out the flesh into a blender but save the melon shells which you use as soup plates. Add all the other ingredients and blend until smooth. If the melon shells do not stand upright on their own cut a sliver off the bottom and if this fails place them in soup dishes. Pour the soup into the four shells and place in a fridge until needed. There are different types of melon so choose one you like. The mint jelly is not the fruit variety but the type you use with lamb.

Cartoon Cook Book... for Men

"I also like my soup to have body"

Stilton and Celery Soup

Stilton is one of my favourite cheeses so when I was served Stilton soup in a small restaurant in Wales I was keen to get the recipe. Most cooks when praised about their endeavours are happy to part with their recipes but I had no success on this occasion as the chef refused to part with it. Some time later I found this recipe in a magazine which, with a few modifications, made a soup which is very moreish. Served with good quality bread and butter it is delicious.

metric	*Ingredients*	*imperial*
40g	butter	1½ oz
4	sticks of celery (15cm/6inch)	4
3tbsp	self raising flour	3tbsp
300ml	milk	½ pint
1	chicken stock cube	1
225g	Stilton cheese	8oz

Method

Trim and chop the celery and cook in the butter in a saucepan for about 5 minutes when it should have softened. Stir in the flour and cook gently for 1 minute. Remove from the heat and gradually stir in the milk and 600ml (1 pint) of water then crumble in the chicken cube. You should aim to make a paste of the flour with a small amount of the milk which you gradually dilute to avoid lumps - this is not important if you have a blender which you use as described below. Return to the stove, bring to the boil then cover and simmer for about 15 minutes on very low heat so that it does not boil over. Gradually stir in the crumbled Stilton until melted. Pour in a blender and mix until smooth. Serve immediately or pour back in the saucepan ready to be heated later.

Notes

Blending is not essential but if you leave it out make sure you mix the milk slowly into the flour so there are no lumps. You can use blue or white Stilton but I prefer the blue for its stronger flavour.

French Onion Soup

Some years ago, on a winter holiday break, my wife and I arrived late at our small hotel in Paris which served only breakfast so we went out in search of something to eat. As it was a Sunday we found most places closed but eventually came across one which looked nice and had a very reasonably priced menu displayed outside. We were shown to an attractively laid table but much to our concern were given a menu with prices about three times those shown outside. After much difficulty and debate the waiter understood and led us to another room in the restaurant where we were presented with the first menu we had seen. We had a superb meal at an excellent price which shows that even in the centre of Paris you can eat well and cheaply if you are prepared to look around. The highlight of the meal was the starter of French onion soup which was a meal in itself.

metric	*Ingredients*	*imperial*
675g	onions	1½ lb
3tsp	sugar	3tsp
1tsp	soy sauce	1tsp
2	beef stock cubes	2
100g	Gruyère cheese	4oz
2tbsp	vegetable oil	2tbsp
pinch	salt	pinch
pinch	pepper	pinch
1	stick French bread	1

Method

Peel and slice the onions and fry for about 10 minutes in the oil in a large saucepan until well browned. Add the sugar and continue to cook stirring carefully for about another 10 minutes when the sugar should be caramelised. You must be very careful that the onions and sugar brown but do not burn. Add the soy sauce, salt, pepper and the stock cubes with 600ml (1 pint) of water, bring to the boil and then reduce the heat to simmer for about 30 minutes with the lid on. Cut the French loaf up into 2½ cm (1 inch) slices and toast under the grill. Pour the soup into ovenproof bowls and float the bread slices on top. Grate the cheese and sprinkle on to the bread - any excess can be sprinkled into the soup. Put the bowls under the grill until the cheese has melted then serve.

Notes

You can eat the soup with a spoon and fork to tear up the bread or as I do, cut the bread into pieces with a knife and fork before serving. Instead of French bread you can use crusty rolls with the bottoms removed. I have used Cheddar cheese in this recipe but it does not work so well as it becomes stringy. This recipe takes a little care as it is important not to let the onions and sugar burn.

Carrot Soup

Of all the ready prepared products on supermarket shelves, soups in my view come closest in quality to those made at home. Manufacturers have spent enormous sums of money in support of their branded soup so you would expect them to have got it right. Canned soups are so good that I have been known to cheat by serving them to guests disguised by the addition of some fresh vegetables. With recipes such as the one below, which is almost as simple to make as opening a can there is rarely any need to cheat - guests will appreciate much more something you have made yourself. This soup is tasty and has a most attractive colour.

metric	*Ingredients*	*imperial*
1	*small onion*	*1*
25g	*butter*	*1oz*
225g	*potato*	*8oz*
450g	*carrots*	*1lb*
1	*chicken stock cube*	*1*
pinch	*salt*	*pinch*
pinch	*pepper*	*pinch*
1tsp	*vegetable oil*	*1tsp*

Method

Peel and chop the onion, potato and carrots. Fry the onion in the butter and oil in a pan until soft and tender. Add all the other ingredients to the pan with 600ml (1 pint) of water. Bring to the boil and simmer for 10-15 minutes by which time the potato and carrots should be soft. Pour into a blender and mix until smooth. Serve immediately or pour back into the pan ready to be heated later.

Notes

A little milk or single cream can be added to thin the soup as required. The original recipe called for chicken stock which is fine if you happen to have such a thing in your kitchen but since I, like most home cooks do not, I use stock cubes which can be bought at any food store. Stock is the liquid made by stewing chicken and meat bones to use as the basis for soups. In the old days a thrifty cook would almost always make stock from the carcass of a chicken but housewives will tell you that today stock cubes are more often than not used instead yet few cookery books ever mention them.

Curried Parsnip Soup

This soup is very easy to make and can be used as a starter before almost any main course. As you would expect it goes well with curries and other spicy dishes but it also can be served before many other main courses. I first tasted curried soup at a dinner party with friends but the hostess refused to give me the recipe so what follows derives from trial and error on my part.

metric	Ingredients	imperial
1	small onion	1
450g	parsnips	1lb
25g	butter	1oz
1	beef cube	1
½ tsp	chilli powder	½ tsp
pinch	salt	pinch
pinch	pepper	pinch
1 tsp	vegetable oil	1 tsp

Method

Peel and chop the parsnips into small cubes. Peel and chop the onion and fry with the parsnips in the oil and butter for about five minutes in a large saucepan. Add all the other ingredients and 600ml (1 pint) of hot water. Bring to the boil and simmer on low heat for fifteen minutes. Place the contents of the saucepan in a blender and blend until smooth. The soup should be thick and ready to serve but can be diluted and extra salt, pepper or chilli powder can be added to taste.

Notes

If you are serving a main dish which requires a lot of attention this is the ideal starter. Prepare the soup well in advance and leave in the saucepan ready for reheating when required.

Mint Pea Soup

Some soups, especially those which involve cheese, are very filling which make them unsuitable for use before substantial main courses. This soup is light with a pleasant taste and attractive green colour. It can also be served cold so is useful as a starter when the weather conditions demand something cool and light.

metric	Ingredients	imperial
450g	minted frozen peas	1lb
50g	butter	2oz
1	onion medium sized	1
600ml	milk	1 pint
1	chicken stock cube	1
1tsp	sugar	1tsp
pinch	salt	pinch
pinch	pepper	pinch
1tbsp	mint jelly	1tbsp
300ml	natural yohgurt	½ pint

Method

Peel and coarsely chop the onion then fry in the butter in a large saucepan for about ten minutes when it should be soft. Add the peas, milk, stock cube, sugar, salt, pepper and 300ml (½ pint) of hot water. Bring to the boil, reduce the heat and simmer for about ten minutes. While waiting, stir the mint jelly into the yoghurt in a bowl until it has mixed well. When it is ready pour the contents of the saucepan into a blender and process until smooth. Pour the soup into warm serving dishes and divide the yoghurt mixture equally between them. Give each bowl a light stir and serve immediately with bread and butter.

Notes

If you are slow with the blending the soup will cool and the yoghurt cools it even further. If you want your soup nice and hot return it to the saucepan after blending and reheat before adding the yoghurt. The mint jelly is not the fruit variety but the type you use with roast lamb - it can be bought at shops and supermarkets.

Salmon and Lemon Pâté

This is an excellent light starter to serve when entertaining guests especially if you are planning a heavy or complicated main course. It can be made well in advance and placed in a fridge until required. Served with buttered light crispbread slices it rarely fails to please.

metric	Ingredients	imperial
200g	salmon tinned	7½ oz
150g	cream cheese low fat	5oz
2tbsp	salad cream	2tbsp
1tbsp	tomato purée	1tbsp
1tbsp	lemon juice	1tbsp
pinch	black pepper	pinch

Method

Drain the salmon and remove any bones and skin - there is no need to go to undue lengths to remove them completely. Put all the ingredients in a basin and stir together with a large spoon until completely mixed. The back of the spoon can be used quite effectively to disperse small lumps of cheese or salmon to give an evenly coloured pink mixture. Turn out into four small ramekin dishes making sure that the tops of the dishes are not smeared with dribs of pâté which spoil the appearance. If necessary wipe clean with a kitchen towel. Cover with cling film and place in a fridge until required.

Notes

The original recipe specified fresh lemon juice but I find it so much easier to use the bottled version bought from my local supermarket. You can put all the ingredients in a blender. While this works well I found it tedious washing the blender afterwards so I prefer mixing by hand with a spoon. A ramekin is a small dish for baking and serving an individual portion of food but any small dish will do.

Cartoon Cook Book... for Men

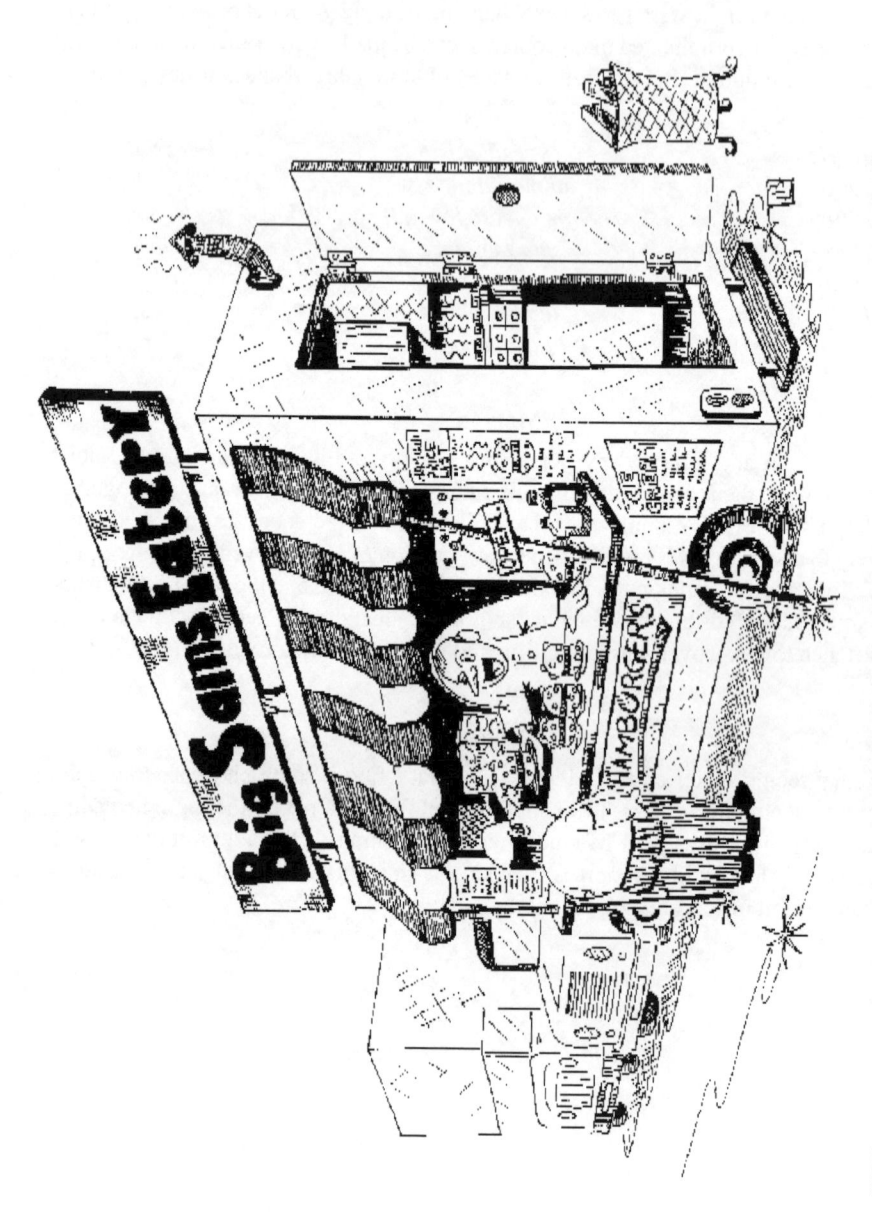

"Try my hamburgers, you'll never get better"

Taramasalata

I like to think that I am adventurous when it comes to food and willing to experiment with new dishes particularly when eating out. However if I am tired and in need of a good meal I refuse to take the risk of trying something new, especially when eating in a restaurant which is not familiar to me. If it is a Greek restaurant I usually choose taramasalata followed by moussaka which can be relied on more often than not. Taramasalata is easy to make from the recipe below and although I like it very much, not everyone is keen on its fishy taste.

metric	**Ingredients**	*imperial*
225g	*cod roe*	*8oz*
1	*small potato*	*1*
1	*garlic clove*	*1*
4tbsp	*lemon juice*	*4tbsp*
1tsp	*vegetable oil*	*1tsp*

Method

Cook the potato by boiling or in a microwave the latter being easier - if you have used the microwave you can peel the cooked potato like an orange by holding it under cold water. Peel and chop the garlic very finely. Place the potato, garlic, cod roe, lemon juice and oil in a large basin and mash together until you have a smooth paste. Add more water if necessary to get the texture of whipped cream. Serve with hot toast.

Notes

This starter can be left in a fridge until you are ready to serve it. I have found that a blender does not work so well with this recipe. If you are not to sure you will like the taste you can buy some at a supermarket to try before making it yourself.

Guacamole

Avocados also called alligator pears because of their rough leathery skin have an oily flesh which is delicate in flavour. Many recipes involve stuffing avocados with a variety of ingredients such as prawns, tuna and cheese but in most cases the fine flavour is overpowered and lost. The Mexicans seem to have got it right with guacamole - in this famous appetiser the other ingredients enhance the flavour of the avocado.

metric	*Ingredients*	*imperial*
1	*avocado*	*1*
2tbsp	*tomato purée*	*2tbsp*
1	*onion small*	*1*
1tsp	*chilli sauce*	*1tsp*
1tsp	*ground coriander*	*1tsp*
1	*garlic clove small*	*1*
1tbsp	*lemon juice*	*1tbsp*
pinch	*salt*	*pinch*
pinch	*pepper*	*pinch*

Method

When you buy the avocado press it gently to make sure it is ripe - cut in two, remove the stone and scrape the flesh away from the skin and place in a bowl. Peel and grate the onion until you have about a teaspoonful. Peel the garlic and crush in a press or by chopping and pressing with the back of a spoon or knife. Mix all the ingredients in the bowl using a fork or by placing in a blender. Spoon into small ramekin dishes and leave in the fridge to chill before serving with toast, crisp bread or pitta bread.

Notes

Be careful that you do not overdo the onion or garlic as these can obscure the taste of the avocado. This is useful starter to use with more bland main courses.

Stuffed Aubergines

Aubergines also known as eggplants are fruits which are treated as vegetables - although freely available in stores in this country they are not commonly used. They are featured strongly in Mediterranean cooking because of their versatility - they easily absorb the different flavours of the other ingredients in a dish, their meaty texture make them a useful vegetable substitute for meat and the purple skin adds to the visual appeal and flavour of a dish. Recipes for stuffed aubergines can be found in many cookery books - this one taken from a book on Mediterranean cooking has been modified to make it easier to prepare.

metric	Ingredients	imperial
2	aubergines	2
2	onions medium sized	2
2	garlic cloves	2
400g	tomatoes chopped canned	14oz
50g	sultanas	2oz
2tsp	allspice	2tsp
2tsp	sugar	2tsp
4tbsp	olive oil	4tbsp
2tbsp	lemon juice	2tbsp

Method

Switch on the oven to 200°C. Peel and finely chop the onion and garlic and put to one side. Cut the aubergines in half lengthwise and scoop out most of the flesh with a spoon being careful not to break the skin. Put the flesh to one side. Brush the inside of the aubergine shells using half of the oil then place on a baking tray and cook in the oven once it has come up to temperature for 20 minutes. Fry the onion and garlic in the remaining oil in a saucepan for about 5 minutes by which time it should be soft. Chop the aubergine flesh into small chunks and add to the saucepan with the tomatoes, sultanas, allspice, sugar and the lemon juice. Cook on medium heat with the lid on for about 15 minutes with an occasional stir. Remove the baked shells from the oven and carefully spoon in the cooked mixture then serve one shell for each person together with good bread and butter. If you have carefully filled the shells you will have some of the mixture over. From a presentational point of view it is best if the mixture does not spill on to the plate but if you are serving yourself you can eat the excess on the plate alongside the shell. I usually eat all the shell and its contents except the stalk.

Notes

Throughout this book you will see the direction to preheat the oven -this tells you to switch on the oven early so that when the time comes to put in the dish the oven is up to temperature. Remember also that the cooking times are given as a guide as the rate of cooking will depend on the condition and type of cooker. It is always best to serve hot food on plates which have been warmed in the oven or in the microwave.

Leeks and Ham with Cheese Sauce

In the dark and cold of winter it is nice to pamper yourself by spending a weekend in the luxury and warmth of a good hotel. Much of the success of your stay will depend on the quality of the food provided by the hotel and in this respect I have usually been lucky. Some years ago I stayed at a small hotel in West Wales which was noted for its food and I was not disappointed. One starter I had was delicious and so simple that I made it as soon as I returned home using the recipe below.

metric	**Ingredients**	*imperial*
4	*leeks*	*4*
100g	*ham*	*4oz*
50g	*butter*	*2oz*
50g	*flour*	*2oz*
50g	*Cheddar cheese*	*2oz*
625ml	*milk*	*1 pint*
pinch	*salt*	*pinch*
pinch	*pepper*	*pinch*

Method

Cut off the bottom and leafy top of each of the leeks to leave about five inches in length. Remove the outer covers if they are marked or stained. Slit the leeks on one side only with a sharp knife for about three quarters of their length and place in a saucepan in salted water then bring to the boil and simmer for about 25 minutes. While waiting for the leeks to cook make the cheese sauce.

Grate the cheese on to a plate. Melt the butter in a saucepan, stir in the flour and cook for one minute on low heat. Remove the pan from the stove and gradually add the milk stirring well between each addition. Return the pan to the heat and bring the sauce to the boil stirring continuously until the sauce thickens. Take off the stove and stir in the cheese, salt and pepper until the sauce is smooth.

Remove the leeks when cooked from the pan being careful that they do not fall apart and let any water drain from them. Finally wrap the ham around the leeks and pour over the cheese sauce. Serve with bread and butter.

Notes

You can use margarine instead of butter to make the cheese sauce if you prefer. The amount of cheese sauce made according to this recipe gives you more than enough but it is better to have too much than too little. If you want to make it easy on yourself you can cheat by buying cheese granules in a shop or supermarket which can be made into a sauce by just adding hot water. Certainly if this is one of the first recipes you try and you are new to cooking I recommend you buy the granules. The amount of ham required depends on its thickness as the thinner it has been cut the less you will need to wrap around the leeks.

Chicken Lemons

This first course is ideal when you want something special to impress friends - essentially it is a chicken pâté but it is served in a novel way. Filling the lemon shells can be a little messy if you are not careful but on the occasion that presentation is important this recipe is well worth consideration. It also has the advantage that it can be made well in advance and left in the fridge until required.

metric	*Ingredients*	*imperial*
4	lemons	4
100g	cream cheese	4oz
225	cooked chicken	8oz
2tsp	sugar	2tsp
1tsp	mixed dried herbs	1tsp
pinch	salt	pinch
pinch	pepper	pinch

Method

Slice about one third off the top of each lemon and use a knife and spoon to remove the flesh from both pieces to form a container and lid. Press the flesh through a sieve and keep the juice. Carefully shave thin slices off the bottom of the larger part of each lemon until they will stand upright on their own. Put two tablespoons of the juice in a blender with all the other ingredients and process until smooth. Spoon the mixture from the blender into the lemon shells, clean any smears and dribbles away with a paper tissue, put the lids back on and serve when required. Provide your guests with a knife each so that they can spread the pâté on hot buttered toast.

Notes

Removing the flesh from the lemons is not easy until you develop the knack - it is like "peeling an orange" from the inside. You must be careful not to pierce the skin but if you do you can plug any holes with small bits of a cheese such as Cheddar pressed to shape. It is usually not worth cooking fresh chicken - you can buy it already cooked or use leftovers but do not bother with scraps of poor quality as they will spoil the flavour. Remember with this and other recipes that the quantities have been converted from metric to imperial as closely as possible and then rounded up so sometimes the amounts do not seem to correspond with each other. As you can see above 4 ounces of cheese corresponds to 100 grams whereas 8 ounces of chicken is equivalent to 225 grams not 200.

Leek Soufflé

If you want to impress yourself and your friends this is the starter for you. I was told that soufflés are difficult to make so imagine my surprise and delight when I got this recipe right the first time. If I can do it I am sure most people can. Follow the directions carefully and read the notes at the end of the recipe before you start. The end result has a light delicate flavour and provided you like the taste of leeks is the ideal choice to proceed a substantial main course. Since the soufflé is somewhat fiddly, make sure the main course is already prepared or very easy to make.

metric	*Ingredients*	*imperial*
450g	leeks	1lb
2	garlic cloves	2
15g	butter	½ oz
150ml	milk	¼ pint
3	eggs	3
1tbsp	self raising flour	1tbsp
½ tsp	salt	½ tsp
½ tsp	pepper	½ tsp
2tbsp	vegetable oil	2tbsp

Method

Preheat the oven to 220°C. Using a small amount of vegetable oil on a piece of kitchen tissue grease the inside of 4 small ramekin or soufflé dishes or one large pudding dish about 18cm by 7cm (7 inch by 3 inch). Separate the egg yolks and whites. Chop the leeks into about half inch lengths removing the leafy part and the root end. Peel and chop the garlic and fry with the leeks in the oil in a saucepan for about 5 minutes. Add 3 tablespoons of hot water and cook for a further 10 minutes until the leeks are soft. Place the contents of the saucepan in a processor or blender until a smooth purée is obtained. Melt the butter in a saucepan, stir in the flour and heat for a few minutes. Remove from the heat and gradually stir in the milk. Return to the stove and heat gently with constant stirring until the mixture thickens. Beat in the egg yolks, leek purée, salt and pepper until the mixture is smooth and lump free. Whisk the egg whites until they are so thick that peaks formed by lifting out the whisk keep their shape and do not resettle then fold in to the leek mixture. Pour into the greased dish or dishes and bake for 20 minutes by which time the soufflés should be risen and golden brown. Serve immediately with French bread and butter.

Notes

Weighing 15g (½ oz) is almost impossible so judge the amount visually by cutting a piece from a packet of butter of known weight. An electric whisk is almost essential for this recipe as whisking by hand can be tedious and seems to take forever. Folding the whites into the mixture is a way of saying stir gently so that the air remains trapped and the soufflé does not deflate - use a large spoon and an up and over movement. To separate an egg, break against the side of a dish and by holding the long axis vertical allow the white to fall into the dish. Keep pouring the yolk from half eggshell to half eggshell until all the white has separated. The puffed up appearance of a soufflé does not hang around long so serve it on a hot plate as soon as it comes out of the oven. The main reasons for soufflé failures are the oven not being at the correct temperature, opening the oven door too early or closing it with a bang. When ready the soufflé should be brown and firm. Big soufflés are often more successful as they retain the heat longer but small individual dishes are more attractive to serve. For the first time perhaps you should try making one large soufflé.

Cartoon Cook Book… for Men

Roasted Peppers

This recipe is so simple that you will be surprised how good the end product tastes. I found it in a well known quality cookery book - it was one of the few recipes I tried as most of the others seemed complicated and fussy.

metric	**Ingredients**	*imperial*
4	red peppers	*4*
4	tomatoes	*4*
50g	anchovy fillets canned	*2oz*
8 dessert spoons	olive oil	*8 dessert spoons*
small amount	pepper	*small amount*

Method

Preheat the oven to 180°C. Cut the peppers in half through the stalk and remove the seeds with a sharp knife to produce eight "cups" Pour boiling water over the tomatoes, leave for a few minutes to cool then peel off the skins. Cut the tomatoes into quarters and place two quarters in each pepper cup and place on a lightly greased roasting tray. Peel and chop the garlic cloves and divide equally between the peppers. Add one anchovy fillet, cut into small pieces using a scissors, to each pepper. Finally add one dessert spoon of olive oil to each cup and sprinkle with a small amount of pepper. Place the tray in the oven and bake for 50 to 60 minutes. Serve with French bread and butter.

Notes

The stalks are not edible but should be left on the peppers so that the cups maintain their shape - they can be left on the plate to be discarded. Each 50g (2oz) can of anchovies contains about eight fillets. If there are more, the extra can be divided equally between the eight pepper cups.

Glamorgan Sausages

If you enjoy cheese and onion sandwiches you will like this traditional Welsh recipe as these sausages do not contain meat but are made from bread, cheese and onions, the staple diet of the poor in days gone by. The original recipe of which this is a slight modification, recommends serving the sausages as a main course with chips or creamed potatoes and peas but in my view they are more suitable served with French bread as a starter or as a light lunch.

metric	Ingredients	imperial
2	eggs	2
1	onion small	1
150g	breadcrumbs fresh	5oz
75g	cheddar cheese	3oz
½ tsp	mixed herbs	½ tsp
½ tsp	mustard powder	½ tsp
pinch	salt	pinch
pinch	pepper	pinch
25g	breadcrumbs crisp	1oz
25g	flour plain	1oz
2tbsp	vegetable oil	2tbsp

Method

Peel and chop the onion as finely as possible. Grate the cheese and mix with the onion, fresh breadcrumbs, herbs, mustard, salt and pepper in a large bowl. Separate the yolk from the white of one the eggs, beat into the second egg then add slowly to the cheese mixture, stirring thoroughly. Beat the separated egg white until frothy. Form the cheese mixture into eight balls with your hands and roll into the flour on a plate. Dip the sausages into the egg white and roll into the crisp breadcrumbs on a plate. Fry in the oil in a frying pan replenishing the oil as necessary. Alternatively immerse the sausages in a deep fryer or chip pan for a few minutes until the coating is crisp and brown.

Notes

Five ounces (150 grammes) of breadcrumbs are equivalent to about three thick slices of bread. Crumb the bread by tearing it into pieces a slice at a time and place in a blender. To separate the egg break against the side of a bowl and by holding the long axis vertical, allow the white to fall into a small soup dish. Keep pouring the yolk from half eggshell to half eggshell until all the white has separated. The crisp breadcrumbs can be bought from a local store or supermarket. If you have difficulty getting the breadcrumbs to adhere to the sausages pat them in with your fingers.

Deep Fried Camembert

This recipe was a real pig when I first tried it but since deep fried Camembert cheese makes a fine starter I persevered and after much trial and error produced the recipe below - it works every time for me so with a little care it should for you. Most cookery books will tell you to coat the cheese wedges with flour, egg and breadcrumbs then put in the freezer until required when the cheese is taken out and immersed in hot fat for a specified time. Getting the timing right is the problem - I usually ended up presenting the cheese to my guests with the centres still frozen or worse having the cheese melt and fall apart in the hot fat. Can you imagine what it feels like to have the cheese disintegrate when your friends are waiting to be served!!!

metric	Ingredients	imperial
4	Camembert wedges	4
1tbsp	flour	1tbsp
1	egg	1
2tbsp	breadcrumbs crisp	2tbsp
pinch	salt	pinch
pinch	pepper	pinch
	oil for deep frying	

Method

To simplify I have divided the recipe into three stages -

Beat the egg in a cup and place the flour and breadcrumbs on two plates. Add the salt and pepper to the flour. Roll each cheese wedge into the flour until coated then dip into the beaten egg and roll in the breadcrumbs patting if necessary to make sure that they adhere. Place in the freezer until solid or until required.

At least 4 hours before you wish to serve take the wedges out of the freezer and deep fry in hot oil for one minute. A basket in a chip pan is ideal for this. The oil is hot enough when a piece of bread dropped in starts to bubble and crisp. If serving the cheese in the evening I usually carry out this stage in the morning.

During the day the cheese will come up to room temperature so the last stage is simple. Place the cheese on a plate in a microwave on full power until you see one of the wedges pop as the molten cheese breaks through the coating. Serve immediately retaining the popped wedge for yourself. Serve with cranberry sauce, a few lettuce leaves as garnish and French bread and butter.

Notes

If you have got it right and there is no reason why you should not, the warm cheese should ooze out on to the plate when you cut it. For a starter serve one wedge per person, two for a light lunch with bread. For this recipe I use "golden breadcrumbs" and cranberry sauce bought from a shop or supermarket.

Garlic Mushrooms

I have often ordered garlic mushrooms in restaurants and been disappointed to receive mushrooms coated in batter with the garlic in an accompanying sauce dip. In this recipe the mushrooms are fried in garlic and butter so that the flavours are absorbed into the flesh which in my view is much more palatable.

metric	*Ingredients*	*imperial*
200g	*mushrooms*	*8oz*
3	*garlic cloves*	*3*
1	*green chilli*	*1*
4tbsp	*olive oil*	*4tbsp*
2tsp	*butter*	*2tsp*
pinch	*salt*	*pinch*

Method

Peel the skin off the mushrooms using your fingers or a knife - the mushrooms should then be clean and white. Chop to cherry size and wash in water before putting in a saucepan with the butter, salt and olive oil. Peel the garlic cloves, deseed the chilli and chop both finely and add to the pan. Fry for a few minutes on high heat spooning the oil and butter over the mushrooms until they soften and appear to shrink. Serve immediately with good quality bread.

Notes

Do not bother measuring out the butter - I have suggested two teaspoons to give you a rough idea of the amount required. Do not confuse green chillies with green peppers - they are both types of capsicum but the latter are about ten times the size and have a much milder flavour. Some books suggest treating green chillies with care and recommend wearing gloves, working in a well ventilated area and caution against rubbing your eyes after contact. I am careful with my eyes but have never found the need to take the other precautions.

Kipper Fish Cakes

Kipper fish cakes are so tasty they deserve a more attractive name but be that as it may, they make an excellent starter or with salad a delicious high tea. The boiled egg, kippers and potatoes provide an unusual combination of flavours which go well together.

metric	Ingredients	imperial
200g	kippers	7oz
450g	potatoes	1lb
1	egg	1
1tsp	grated onion	1tsp
1tsp	mustard powder	1tsp
1tbsp	milk	1tbsp
2tbsp	vegetable oil	2tbsp
pinch	ground nutmeg	pinch
small amount	flour	small amount

Method

Cook the potatoes in a microwave until soft - it usually takes about 10-15 minutes depending on power. Allow to cool or by immersing in cold water, then peel and mash with a fork in a large bowl. In the meantime, cook the kippers according to the instructions on the packet - for boil-in-the-bag usually 20 minutes in boiling water. When cooked drain off the excess liquid. While waiting for the potatoes and kippers to finish cooking simmer the egg in boiling water for about 4 minutes by which time it should be hard. Remove the shell and chop finely. Peel and grate the onion until you have about one teaspoonful. Add to the potatoes all the other ingredients - the kippers, chopped egg, grated onion, mustard powder, nutmeg and milk and beat together with a fork until completely mixed. Form the mixture into eight rissoles with your hands, dab in the flour until evenly coated then fry in the oil in a large frying pan for about 5 minutes on each side when they should be browned.

Notes

If you prefer you can peel, chop and cook the potatoes in boiling water until soft - it usually takes about 15-20 minutes depending on how small you have chopped the potato. I prefer to use a microwave as it does not require so much watching. If you do not have mustard powder you can use made up paste instead.

Sardine Triangles

Over the years I have collected recipes in two ways - I have asked for the recipe of a dish I have enjoyed at a friend's house or at a restaurant or I have seen a recipe in a book or magazine which attracts my interest. The unusual combination of sardines and peanut butter aroused my interest in this starter but there were other aspects of the recipe which I did not like so I have changed them. Remember if there is something about a recipe you do not like provided it is not essential, change it.

metric	*Ingredients*	*imperial*
8	*slices of bread*	*8*
100g	*canned sardines in tomato sauce*	*4oz*
3	*eggs*	*3*
50g	*butter*	*2oz*
1tbsp	*peanut butter*	*1tbsp*
150ml	*milk*	*¼ pint*
pinch	*salt*	*pinch*
pinch	*pepper*	*pinch*

Method

Cut the crusts off the bread. Butter the slices with the peanut butter then the sardines mashed together. Beat one of the eggs in a bowl with the salt, pepper, half the butter and two tablespoons of milk. Heat in a microwave for about 30 seconds until the egg begins to rise, remove and stir before reheating for another 30 seconds by which time the egg should be scrambled. Finely chop the egg then spread over the bread with the sardines and peanut butter. Press the eight slices of bread together firmly to form four sandwiches then cut neatly into eight triangles. Beat the other two eggs with the rest of the milk in a shallow bowl. Dip the triangles into the eggs and fry on both sides in the remaining butter in a large frying pan until brown. Serve alone or decorate with salad.

Notes

Make sure the eggs are mixed well to coat the bread so that they sink well in. Remember that some people are allergic to peanut butter so check before serving. Presentation is important so make sure the triangles are neatly cut. This is a very filling starter so match it with a light main course.

Smoked Salmon and Scrambled Eggs

This combination of salmon and eggs goes down well for breakfast but also can be used to make a very tasty starter. Smoked salmon is rather expensive but if you like its taste in combination with creamy scrambled eggs it can be worth the extra cost. Scrambling eggs in a microwave is easier than heating them in a saucepan as it is quicker and the washing up is easier.

metric	*Ingredients*	*imperial*
100g	smoked salmon	*4oz*
2	eggs	*2*
25g	butter	*1oz*
2tbsp	milk	*2tbsp*
pinch	salt	*pinch*
pinch	pepper	*pinch*

Method

Cut the salmon into small pieces. Put the eggs, butter, milk, salt and pepper into a glass bowl and whisk together with a fork until smooth. Cook in the microwave until you see the eggs beginning to set at the edges of the bowl. Take the bowl out of the microwave and stir again to incorporate the set egg. Add the smoked salmon and cook again until the eggs are set but soft. Break up the salmon and egg mixture with a fork and serve on triangles of buttered toast.

Notes

If you do not have a microwave follow the directions above but cook the eggs in a saucepan on the stove. You can buy ready made vol-au-vent cases at stores and supermarkets which can be cooked in the oven and filled with the salmon and egg mixture to give an alternative method of presentation. This recipe will give you enough to fill about sixteen small cases. You can buy smoked salmon trimmings which are ideal for this recipe.

Onion Bhaji

This is my own version of this popular Indian starter. The original recipe did not use egg but I found that it gives a better texture to the end-product and makes the mixture easier to handle. This is an ideal starter before a curry or other spicy main course. It is usually served in Indian restaurants with yoghurt and mint sauce which is an ideal accompaniment. See page 96 for the recipe.

metric	Ingredients	imperial
2	onions medium	2
1	egg	1
150g	gram flour	5oz
1tsp	salt	1tsp
½ tsp	chilli powder	½ tsp
¼ tsp	tumeric	¼ tsp
¼ tsp	baking powder	¼ tsp
2tbsp	vegetable oil	2tbsp

Method

Break the egg into a cup to ensure that no shell fragments are included. Weigh out the flour and sieve into a bowl. Add all the other ingredients plus 100ml (4floz) of water. Stir to form a batter of cream like consistency. Peel and chop the onions and add to the batter. Mix in as much onion as you can so the mixture is not too wet. Chop more onions if necessary. Heat the oil in a frying pan and add the mixture in tablespoon portions. Fry one side until brown then flip over with a spatula and cook the other side. Press down firmly to ensure that any surplus batter oozes from the bhaji and cooks thoroughly. Add more oil as necessary.

Notes

This mixture makes eight medium sized bhajias. The gram flour which can be bought at Indian stores should be kept in a glass jar. I found from experience that gram flour left in an opened packet can become infested with small insects. The proportions in this recipe can be varied to suit your taste I prefer to chop the onion finely and add as much as I can otherwise the bhajias can resemble mini omelettes.

Yorkshire Pudding and Curry Sauce

Bradford in Yorkshire can justifiably claim to be the curry capital of Great Britain as it has many quality Indian and Pakastani restaurants. Indeed, while travelling on business in the area I have driven an extra hundred miles to enjoy the food at one of its restaurants. No - it was not one of the up market variety which charges exorbitant prices for its fare but a rather down at heel transport cafe type restaurant where the food was superb - knives and forks were not supplied, chappatis were used to scoop up the curry. However, this recipe stems from a visit to Newcastle not Bradford where in a vegetarian Indian restaurant I tried by chance a starter which consisted of little puddings covered with curry. The crisp puddings soaked in the mild sauce were delicious but despite my efforts I have failed to find anything like them served in Indian restaurants or described in cookery books - chappatis, parathas, puris and nans in plenty but no little puddings. Then I realised that the nearest thing to it were Yorkshire puddings so now I often serve as a starter individual Yorkshire puddings with a curry sauce. You can of course make the puddings and the curry sauce but to make a simple starter I buy both of them at stores or supermarkets. The Yorkshire puddings require only a few minutes in the oven and the curry sauce a similar time to heat in a saucepan or a microwave. I like my sauce to be mild and thin like gravy but there is a wide range from which to choose.

Cartoon Cook Book... for Men

SATISFACTION - IN THE MAIN ?

Someone once said that eating books is bad for you because they can be difficult to digest. Hopefully you will be satisfied with the personal approach to food found in these pages and will find the recipes and their end-products easy to assimilate. One criticism of this book is perhaps that it concentrates too much on chicken and pays less attention to beef and lamb for main courses. In my view the strong and distinctive flavours of these meats require very little embellishment whereas the bland flavour of chicken is enhanced by the addition of herbs and spices. The natural flavours of beef, lamb and pork are so delicious that it seems almost a sacrilege to do anything other than roast them as in the traditional Sunday lunch a meal, which in my view, can rarely be surpassed. Similarly delicately flavoured fish like Dover sole do not benefit from being smothered in heavy sauces which mask their taste.

When preparing to entertain guests select the main course, the heart of the meal, first and build the rest of the menu around it. Choose a dish you are sure of and preferably something that virtually cooks itself or just requires heating from the freezer. Make sure you get your timing right - by the time you finish the first course, the main course should be ready or require just a few minutes attention. One problem you might have is keeping food hot without it becoming overcooked and dry. If the main dish is ready before time turn the oven down to its lowest setting and cover the dish with aluminium foil to prevent it drying out. Rice and pasta can be kept hot in a colander on a saucepan of hot water simmering on low heat or can be quickly reheated in a microwave oven. Unless desperate do not be tempted to dish up before your guests are ready as it will be much more difficult to keep individual plates warm. It is always preferable to put the dishes on the table so that your guests can help themselves to what they want and can savour the appearance of the food before diving into it. If you entertain a lot you may consider investing in a hot plate food warmer which is attractive enough to place on the dining table. If you do serve up beforehand serve only moderate portions as an overfull plate can put people off. It is also nice to hear your friends ask for more.

After the feast comes the washing up but be resolute in your determination not to keep slipping into the kitchen to reduce the load as it begins to pile up. If you give way it will spoil your own enjoyment of the meal and give your friends the impression that you are trying to get it over as quickly as possible. Pile them up and wash them later, even the next day if necessary.

While there is no need to be conventional it is obvious that certain dishes do not mix well - a pasta starter will not fit well with an Indian main course but less obviously it is important not to serve dishes which do not complement each other or are too much alike for example a starter and main course both served with heavy cream sauces.

The recipes in this book have been planned to provide four good sized portions. If cooking just for yourself or only two people I recommend you stick to the recipe and divide the food when cooked into portions and put those not being used into the freezer for another day.

MENU - MAIN COURSE

Chicken   **Page**
1. Satay. 55
2. Korma. 56
3. Ceylon Curry. 57
4. Javea. 59
5. Ham and Leek Pie. 60
6. Mexican. 61
7. Garlic and Herb Sauce. 62
8. Coronation. 63
9. Honey and Mustard. 64
10. Black Bean Sauce. 65
11. Chow Mein. 66

Beef
1. Peppered Steak. 68
2. Curry. 69
3. Chilli and Beans. 71
4. Pie with Yoghurt. 72

Lamb
1. Honey Roast. 73
2. Moussaka. 74

Pasta and Pizza
1. Lasagne. 77
2. Tagliatelle Carbonara. 79
3. Cannelloni. 80
4. Chilli. 82
5. Polenta Pizza. 83

Fish
1. Tuna and Tomato Penne. 85
2. Salmon Pie. 86
3. Fish and Chips. 87

Chicken Satay

This dish is easy to prepare and is one of the most popular with my friends. I have eaten satay in Singapore but can honestly say that it was no better than that prepared in my own kitchen according to this recipe. This was one of the first recipes I ever collected - by surreptitiously tearing it out of an old magazine lying around in a dentist's waiting room. After much trial an error the recipe has been modified to that reproduced below. Before serving this dish to friends I always ask whether they like the taste of peanut butter and whether they are allergic to it. Fortunately the answer to the first question has always been yes and the second no.

metric	Ingredients	imperial
4	chicken breasts	4
4	garlic cloves	4
3tbsp	soy sauce	3tbsp
2tsp	brown sugar	2tsp
1tsp level	chilli powder	level 1tsp
3tbsp	dessicated coconut	3tbsp
1tbsp	lemon juice	1tbsp
3tbsp	cooking oil	3tbsp
1	onion medium size	1
150g	peanut butter	5oz

Method

Peel and chop the onions and garlic and fry in the oil in a saucepan until soft. Cut the chicken into bite size pieces with a scissors and fry with the onions until brown. Add all the other ingredients with 600ml (1 pint) of hot water to the saucepan. Bring to the boil, then simmer on low heat for 30 minutes with the lid on. The mixture should thicken to a cream like consistency but if for some reason it does not, add to the satay a teaspoon of cornflour in a small amount of cold water. Serve with rice - see later.

Notes.

Chicken breasts are preferable but leftovers or chicken pieces will do. Note that the measure for chilli powder is a level teaspoon - for the other ingredients, making sure the spoon measures are level is not so important. This is because the amount of chilli is critical to the taste. Do not bother squeezing a lemon - buy a bottle of lemon juice from a supermarket.

Chicken Korma

As you will see this recipe is very simple and uses few ingredients, which can all be bought without too much difficulty. The curry paste can be bought at supermarkets but the types you find in Indian shops are preferable.

metric	Ingredients	imperial
1lb	chicken off the bone	450g
4	garlic cloves	4
4tbsp	curry paste mild	4tbsp
1	onion large	1
4tbsp	dessicated coconut	4tbsp
7oz	crème fraiche	200g
2	bananas	2
4tbsp	vegetable oil	4tbsp

Method

Peel and chop the onion and garlic and fry in the oil in a large saucepan until soft. Cut the chicken with a scissors into bite size pieces and fry with onions until brown. Add 400ml (¾ pint) of hot water, the curry paste and the coconut. Bring to the boil, then lower the heat and simmer for 40 minutes with the lid on. If the chicken is already cooked add to the onion and garlic with the curry paste, coconut and water and simmer for only 20 minutes. Then take the saucepan off the heat, and stir in the crème fraiche and the bananas sliced. Serve immediately with rice.

Notes

The crème fraiche gives a rich flavour to the dish but if you prefer you can use 250g (9oz) of canned evaporated milk.

Ceylon Chicken Curry

When you see that this recipe uses eight spices you may ask why bother - is it not easier to make a curry using the paste featured in the recipe for chicken korma? It is but the result is not so tasty. There is no point in wasting time grinding spices when there is a simpler alternative so as an experiment I served a party of friends two curries - one made using the paste the other according to the recipe below. The verdict was unanimous, the curry made with the paste did not have the same depth of flavour.

metric	Ingredients	imperial
450g	chicken off the bone	1lb
4	garlic cloves	4
1	onion large	1
1 inch	ginger root	1 inch
1tsp	fennel	1tsp
2 inch stick	cinnamon	2 inch stick
6	cardamon pods	6
¼ tsp	fenugreek	¼ tsp
2tsp	coriander	2tsp
2tsp	cumin	2tsp
¼ tsp	black pepper	¼ tsp
1tsp level	chilli powder	level 1tsp
½ tsp	tumeric	½ tsp
1tsp	salt	1tsp
4tsp	tomato purée	4tsp
100g	coconut cream	4oz
4tbsp	vegetable oil	4tbsp

Method

Grind the fennel, cinnamon and fenugreek with the seeds from the cardamom pods and put on a plate. Add the coriander, cumin, black pepper, chilli powder, salt, and tumeric. Peel and chop finely the onions and garlic and fry in a large saucepan in the oil until soft. Cut the chicken into bite sized pieces discarding the skin. Fry in the oil and onions until brown. Peel and chop the ginger root and add to the saucepan with the tomato purée, the mixed spices, the coconut cream and 600ml (1 pint) of hot water. Bring to the boil then simmer on low heat with the lid on the saucepan for 40 minutes. The curry should thicken to a creamy consistency but if not add a teaspoon of cornflour in a quarter of a cup of cold water then heat until it does. Serve with rice or chappatis.

Notes

Measure the chilli powder carefully as small variations can affect the heat of the curry. With experience the amount can be adjusted to suit your taste. The amounts of the other

Ceylon Chicken Curry

ingredients are not so critical. To grind the spices I use a small coffee grinder. Chicken breasts are preferable but leftovers can be used - in this case reduce the cooking time to 20 minutes. The spices can be bought at most supermarkets and Indian food stores. The need to buy so many spices may put you off this recipe as your money will be wasted if you do not like the end result but it is worth a try. If you cannot get ginger root and cinnamon bark use instead one teaspoon each of the powdered versions.

Breakfast in bed

Chicken Javea

This dish is typical of the others you will find in the book - it is simple, tasty and uses ingredients readily available in shops and supermarkets. I have called the dish Chicken Javea because I was given the recipe in Javea, Spain by some friends who live there permanently - served with salad and more than a few bottles of wine it made an extremely pleasant meal. Whenever I prepare this dish I am reminded of the sunshine and companionship of that day. No doubt the dish is not Spanish and has a less interesting origin.

metric	*Ingredients*	*imperial*
450g	*chicken off the bone*	*1lb*
450g	*broccoli frozen*	*1lb*
600g	*concentrated chicken soup canned*	*22oz*
225g	*Cheddar cheese*	*8oz*
2tbsp	*salad cream*	*2tbsp*
4 rounds	*bread*	*4 rounds*
120g	*plain crisps*	*4½ oz*
½ tsp	*pepper*	*½ tsp*

Method

Preheat the oven to 190°C. Remove any skin from the chicken and cut into bite size pieces with a scissors and cook in the oven in a casserole for 25 minutes. In the meantime cook the broccoli in salted boiling water for half the recommended time on the packet. Cool and cut in pieces similar in size to the chicken. Pour the soup into a jug, dilute with 300ml (½ pint) of hot water and mix in the pepper and salad cream. Grate the cheese, powder the crisps, crumb the bread and mix together in a large bowl. Once the chicken has cooked, place in a 2 litre (3½ pint) pie dish and add the broccoli. Pour in the soup and cover evenly with the cheese mixture. Bake in the oven for 30 minutes.

Notes

I prefer to use good quality breast of chicken but leftovers from a roast will do. If the chicken is already cooked you must of course ignore the relevant part of the recipe. Powder the crisps by opening the bags and squeezing them hard. A good way to crumb the bread is to break it into small pieces and place in a blender. This dish can be eaten as a main course on its own but is particularly good with salad. One advantage of Chicken Javea is that it can be left in the oven on low heat without spoiling while waiting for guests to arrive.

Chicken Ham and Leek Pie

This recipe is very similar to that for Chicken Javea but it provides quite a differently flavoured dish. For convenience I have repeated the directions in detail.

metric	Ingredients	imperial
450g	chicken off the bone	1lb
2	large leeks	2
4	medium sized potatoes	4
100g	cooked ham	4oz
600g	concentrated chicken soup canned	22oz
225g	Cheddar cheese	8oz
4 rounds	bread	4 rounds
120g	plain crisps	5oz
½ tsp	salt	½ tsp
½ tsp	pepper	½ tsp

Method

Preheat the oven to 190°C. Remove any skin and cut the chicken into bite sized pieces with a scissors. Cook in a casserole in the oven for 25 minutes. Remove the root end and leafy part of the leeks and chop the stems into 1cm (½ inch) circular discs. Cut the discs in half and cook in boiling water for 10 minutes. Peel and slice the potatoes and add to the leeks and cook for a further 10 minutes. Pour the soup into a jug and dilute with 300ml (½ pint) of hot water. Grate the cheese, powder the crisps, crumb the bread and mix together in a large bowl. Once the chicken has cooked place in a 2 litre (3½ pint) pie dish. Cut the ham into small pieces then add to the chicken and sprinkle over the salt and pepper. Pour in the diluted soup and cover evenly with the cheese mixture. Cook in the oven for 30 minutes.

Notes

I prefer to use good quality breast of chicken (4 breasts) but leftovers from a roast will do. If the chicken you are using is already cooked ignore the appropriate part of the recipe. The best way to crumb the bread is to break it into small pieces and place in a blender. Powder the crisps by opening the bags and squeezing them hard. This dish can be eaten on its own as a main course but it is even nicer with a salad.

Mexican Chicken

The attraction of this dish, also called Pollo Mole Poblano, is the unusual combination of chilli and chocolate. Do not be put off by seeing chocolate in a main course as it is the vital ingredient which makes the dish different. The spicy rich flavour is delicious with sweet rice but if you do not have a sweet tooth plain rice is fine.

metric	**Ingredients**	*imperial*
450g	chicken off the bone	1lb
1	onion	1
2	garlic cloves	2
4tbsp	vegetable oil	4tbsp
25g	plain chocolate	1oz
2tsp	tomato purée	2tsp
1tsp	sugar	1tsp
2tbsp	vinegar	2tbsp
1tsp	salt	1tsp
1tsp level	chilli powder	level 1tsp
2	chicken stock cubes	2
½ tsp	cinnamon powder	½ tsp
400g	canned chopped tomatoes	14oz

Method

Preheat the oven to 190°C. Cut the chicken into bite sized pieces and place in a medium sized casserole dish. Peel and chop the onion and garlic cloves and fry in the oil in a saucepan or frying pan until soft. Add the chocolate, tomato purée and sugar and heat until the chocolate has melted. Add 300ml (½ pint) of hot water to the pan and stir so that the mixture can be easily transferred to a blender. Add to the blender the vinegar, salt, chilli powder cinnamon, and tomatoes and sprinkle in the chicken cubes. Blend for a minute or so until the mixture is homogeneus. Pour the mixture from the blender over the chicken in the casserole and cook in the oven for 40 minutes. Serve with sweet rice or plain rice.

Notes

This dish can be left in the oven well over the allotted time so it is ideal when you are not sure when you will be sitting down for your meal or when your starter requires a lot of attention. If you do not have a blender put the onions, garlic and chocolate mixture in a large dish with the other ingredients and stir well before adding to the chicken in the casserole.

Chicken with Garlic and Herb Sauce

If you serve this to your guests and they close their eyes they can easily imagine they are eating a meal in a good class French restaurant as the chicken in garlic and herb cheese sauce is exceptionally good. Yet nothing could be simpler to prepare as you will soon see.

metric	Ingredients	imperial
4	chicken breasts	4
4tbsp	white wine or sherry	4tbsp
100g	garlic and herb cheese	4oz
1tsp	cornflour	1tsp

Method

Remove the skin and cut the chicken lengthwise into finger like pieces. Place in a casserole with the lid on and cook for 25 minutes in a preheated oven at 190°C. Once the chicken has cooked pour the liquid off into a saucepan and keep the chicken warm in the oven. Add the cheese and the wine (or sherry) to the saucepan and stir briskly with a fork until completely mixed. The mixture will probably be thin so thicken by adding the cornflour made up to a paste in about a tablespoon of cold water. Gently heat and stir until the sauce thickens to a cream like consistency. Place the chicken on warmed plates and spoon over the sauce. Serve with buttered new potatoes and a selection of vegetables such as carrots and red and yellow peppers.

Notes

At most stores and supermarkets you will find a well known garlic and herb cheese which is excellent for this recipe. However supermarket own brands are usually cheaper and almost as good. You can use chicken leftovers in this recipe and if you do just warm them in an oven or microwave before adding the sauce. However the recipe is too good to spoil by using scraps of poor quality chicken.

Coronation Chicken

This dish was devised for the Queen's guests at her Coronation lunch in 1953. A cold dish was required as the kitchen facilities at the Westminster school where the meal was served were too small to prepare a hot meal. Originally known as Sauce Elizabeth the dish consists of strips of chicken in a light curry mayonnaise sauce - it can be served cold with salad as part of a buffet or main meal. The version which follows was given to me by a friend and is served hot with rice.

metric	Ingredients	imperial
4	chicken breasts	4
450ml	mayonnaise	15floz
150g	mild curry paste	5oz
1	red pepper	1
1	onion	1
440g	pineapple pieces canned	1lb
2tbsp	vegetable oil	2tbsp
2	garlic cloves	2

Method

Peel and chop the onion and garlic and place in a large saucepan with the oil. Cut the pepper in half and remove the stalk and seeds - chop roughly and fry with the onion and garlic until soft. This usually takes about 5 minutes. Remove the skin and cut the chicken into bite sized pieces with a scissors - fry in the saucepan with the other ingredients until brown. Add the curry paste and the juice from the pineapple pieces made up to 300ml ($^1/_2$ pint) with hot water, bring to the boil and simmer for 30 minutes with the lid on by which time the chicken should be cooked through. You can check by cutting a piece if you are not sure. Finally add the mayonnaise and the pineapple pieces, stir, bring to the boil and serve immediately.

Notes

The curry paste bought at Indian stores is ideal for this recipe. I prefer to use chicken breasts but leftovers can be used - in this case after frying the onion, garlic and pepper simply add the other ingredients and bring to the boil before serving. Weigh the curry paste on to a small plate or by difference that is by weighing the jar and by removing the paste until the weight has been reduced by the required amount. This recipe gives four large helpings but can be stretched to serve six.

Honey and Mustard Chicken

Sometime ago I drove two hundred miles from home to visit friends and was made most welcome with a nice meal and a bottle of wine. The wine was appreciated but what pleased me more was the main course of the meal which was chicken in honey and mustard sauce. The recipe which is reproduced below surprised me by its simplicity. If you have friends coming for a meal at short notice this dish is ideal as all you do is put the ingredients in a casserole and wait for them to cook.

metric	*Ingredients*	*imperial*
4	chicken breasts	*4*
100g	clear honey	*4oz*
100g	German mustard	*4oz*
25g	butter	*1oz*
pinch	chilli powder	*pinch*

Method

Preheat the oven to 190°C. Remove the skin and place the chicken in a casserole with all the other ingredients. Add a tablespoon of water - this small amount is added to give the sauce the right consistency so you can vary this to suit. Put the casserole in the oven with the lid on for 40 minutes stirring once half way through. Serve on warm plates spooning some of the sauce over each chicken breast.

Notes

All the amounts of the ingredients can be varied to suit your taste. I buy the German mustard at a supermarket. I am not sure what this dish would be like with other types of mustard so there is room for you to experiment here. Weighing the honey can be tricky particularly if it is thick. Warm the jar with lid off in a microwave or hot water and weigh by difference - place the jar on the scales and remove a little at a time until the weight has reduced by the correct amount.

Chicken in Black Bean Sauce

Chinese food is not my first choice when I go out for a meal as I find it rather bland and not very filling. Whereas most meals out leave me well satisfied, after Chinese I usually feel like eating more and although this can be a good sign it is not when you are left still feeling hungry. However a meal in a restaurant in Edinburgh some years ago gave me a liking for chicken in black bean sauce so when I found this recipe in a book on Chinese cooking I was keen to try it. It did not disappoint me.

metric	Ingredients	imperial
450g	chicken	1lb
2tbsp	soy sauce	2tbsp
1tbsp	sherry	1tbsp
2	garlic cloves	2
50g	crystallised ginger	2oz
1	red pepper	1
225g	bamboo shoots canned	8oz
160g	black bean sauce	6oz
8	spring onions	8
2tbsp	vegetable oil	2tbsp

Method

Preheat the oven to 180°C. Deseed the pepper, remove the stalk and cut into thin strips about 5cm (2 inches) long. Peel and finely chop the garlic then fry with the pepper in the oil in a pan for a few minutes. Cut the chicken into bite sized pieces and fry in the same pan until brown all over. Now place the contents of the pan in a casserole. Top and tail the spring onions and cut in strips about the same size as the pepper. Add to the casserole with all the other ingredients except the ginger. Cook in the oven for 30 minutes. Cut the ginger in to small pieces and add to the casserole just before serving.

Notes

An advantage of using a casserole is that it can be put on the table so that people can help themselves. It is usual to serve this dish with rice but I think it is particularly good with sweet potatoes - see later. If you use precooked chicken you can cut the time in the oven by about half. Drain the liquid from the bamboo shoots before adding to the casserole.

Chicken Chow Mein

The ingredients listed below are virtually the same as in the original recipe which I found in a magazine but there are a number of differences in the method. In the original, the vegetables had to be added to the pan separately and cooked for varying lengths of time - this seemed tedious so I put them all together in a casserole. Then the chicken and vegetables had to be mixed together with the noodles in the pan but my pan was not big enough to cope so I had to serve them in separate dishes. Finally the noodles were too knotted to mix evenly with the chicken and vegetables on the plate so I cut them with a pair of scissors.

metric	*Ingredients*	*imperial*
150g	chicken	5oz
1	red pepper	1
100g	mange-tout	4oz
6	spring onions	6
15g	fresh coriander	½ oz
4tbsp	soy sauce	4tbsp
2tbsp	sherry	2tbsp
2tsp	clear honey	2tsp
1tbsp	sesame oil	1tbsp
2tbsp	vegetable oil	2tbsp
250g	egg noodles	9oz
pinch	black pepper	pinch

Method

Preheat the oven to 180°C. First prepare the vegetables. Deseed the red pepper and cut it into strips, trim off the ends of the onions and mange-tout and cut to about the same size as the pepper. Wash the cut vegetables in a colander under the tap then place in a casserole. If you are using chicken breasts (you will need two) remove the skin, cut into strips with a scissors and fry in a large saucepan with the vegetable oil until brown. Put the chicken in the casserole add the soy sauce, honey, black pepper and sherry and cook in the oven for 30 minutes with the lid on. Wash and chop the coriander and add to the casserole just before serving. Just before the casserole is due to be taken out of the oven drop the noodles into a large pan of boiling water and continue boiling for 4 minutes. Drain in a colander, snip with a scissors to manageable lengths and toss in the sesame oil in a saucepan. Pour into a dish ready for serving.

Notes

In writing up this recipe I thought I would cut the noodles by half as I like a lot of chicken and vegetables compared to the amount of noodles but I decided to leave the recipe unchanged so you can vary the amounts to suit yourself.

Cartoon Cook Book... for Men

"Beef Wellington"

Peppered Steak

It has been said that most British men on an evening out will order steak, onions and chips followed by apple pie and cream. While I am very partial to apple pie, steak is not my first choice for a meal out. In my view steak is expensive and very much overrated as a culinary experience and I prefer the chef to earn his money by preparing something which I cannot easily cook for myself. Cooking steak is not difficult and the recipe for peppered steak below should not present any problems and provides a meal which is almost as good as my favourite of roast beef with lashings of gravy and vegetables.

metric	*Ingredients*	*imperial*
4	*steaks*	*4*
200g	*crème fraiche*	*7oz*
2	*beef cubes*	*2*
4tbsp	*brandy*	*4tbsp*
2tsp	*butter*	*2tsp*
4tsp	*peppercorns*	*4tsp*
2tbsp	*vegetable oil*	*2tbsp*
1tsp	*cornflour*	*1tsp*

Method

Fry the steaks in the oil according to taste as follows. If you like your steak rare, cook for two to three minutes, turn and repeat on the other side. If you prefer your steak well done repeat as above, then cover with a saucepan lid and continue to cook on a low heat for a further ten minutes - the saucepan lid prevents the steak from drying out. For the sauce crush the peppercorns in a dish with the back of a large spoon or by using a coffee grinder. Place the steaks in the oven to keep warm while you make the sauce. Discard about three quarters of the liquid in the pan and add to the remainder the beef cubes dissolved in 200ml (8 floz) of hot water, the crème fraiche, brandy, butter and crushed peppercorns. Dissolve one teaspoon of cornflour in two tablespoons of cold water and add to the sauce in the pan. Bring to the boil slowly and stir until the sauce thickens. To serve place the steaks on warmed plates and pour over the sauce.

Notes

You will see that I have not specified the size or type of steak as this is a matter of personal preference. The cornflour is added to thicken the sauce. Two teaspoons of butter seems an odd measure but it gives you an idea of the amount to use and avoids the difficulty of weighing such a small amount.

Beef Curry

Beef is not my first choice when I come to make a curry - it can be too chewy, expensive and its taste is masked by the curry so why use it? Chicken is preferable as its bland flavour and soft texture go well with the curry spices. It would be interesting to know how many curries using beef or lamb are ordered in Indian restaurants compared with chicken. However I have included the following recipe for lovers of beef - I do cook it but this curry is not one of my favourites. The recipe is essentially that which I was taught at Indian cookery classes except that I have introduced tomato purée and left out cloves. The smell of cloves has bad memories for me as when I was a child cloves were often used in solution to ease toothache. Also in the original recipe the meat and spices had to be simmered for an hour in the saucepan but even then the beef was too chewy for my liking so I have modified the cooking as shown below.

metric	*Ingredients*	*imperial*
700g	braising beef	1½ lb
1	onion medium sized	1
2tbsp	vegetable oil	2tbsp
3	garlic cloves	3
2.5cm	ginger root	1 inch
¼ tsp	ground turmeric	¼ tsp
¼ tsp	black pepper	¼ tsp
1tsp	salt	1tsp
1½ tsp	coriander	1½ tsp
1½ tsp	cumin	1½ tsp
1tsp	chilli powder	1tsp
3	cardamom pods	3
2.5cm	cinnamon stick	1 inch
¼ tsp	fenugreek	¼ tsp
2tbsp	tomato purée	2tbsp
50g	creamed coconut	2oz
2tsp	malt vinegar	2tsp

Method

Preheat the oven to 160°C. Remove the seeds from the cardamom pods and grind with the cinnamon and the fenugreek. Weigh all the other spices as listed. Peel and chop the onion, the garlic and the ginger and fry in the oil for a few minutes until soft. Cut the beef into bite sized chunks and fry in the saucepan with the onions until brown. Add all the spices, the tomato purée, the vinegar, the coconut and 300ml (½ pint) of hot water. Bring the mixture to the boil, pour into a casserole and place in the oven with the lid on for two hours so that the beef can cook slowly. Stir occasionally and add more hot water if the curry thickens too much. Serve with basmati rice.

Beef Curry Cartoon Cook Book... for Men

Notes

Although the recipe specifies braising beef I often use rump steak from which all traces of fat have been removed as I have a horror of finding a lump of fat or gristle in my mouth. I like my meat to fall apart in my mouth and I am not keen on anything that is too chewy. The recipe lists one inch of ginger root - you need about a teaspoonful when chopped. To grind the cinnamon etc. I use a small coffee grinder. Note the two meanings of the word clove - cloves or bulbs of garlic and the cloves formerly used in dentistry which are dried flower buds.

"Cooking under pressure"

Chilli Beef and Beans

This dish is so easy that it can be embarrassing when friends lick their lips, ask for second helpings then demand the recipe. So what, good food does not depend on its price or on how difficult it is to prepare nor should one be embarrassed if most of the ingredients come from cans. Whether it tastes good should be the main concern. There is one drawback to this recipe - it takes two and a half hours to cook but if you are not in a hurry to rush off somewhere it need not be a problem.

metric	*Ingredients*	*imperial*
1000g	braising steak	2lb
400g	canned chopped tomatoes	14oz
450g	canned mixed beans in mild chilli sauce	1lb
1	green pepper	1
1	onion	1
2	cloves garlic	2
15g	butter	½ oz
1tsp	Worcester sauce	1tsp
1tsp	sugar	1tsp
½ tsp	salt	½ tsp
½ tsp	pepper	½ tsp
1tbsp	vegetable oil	1tbsp

Method

Preheat the oven to 180°C. Peel and chop the garlic finely and the onion roughly and fry in the oil and butter in a large saucepan for a few minutes. Cut the steak into bite sized pieces with a scissors and fry with the onions until browned all over. Pour the contents of the saucepan into a large casserole and add the tomatoes, the sugar, the beans and 100ml (4 floz) of hot water and place in the oven. After one hour deseed and chop the green pepper and add to the casserole with the Worcester sauce, salt and pepper giving the mixture a good stir before cooking for a further one and a half hours. Serve with rice or fried potatoes.

Notes

Minced beef can be used instead of braising steak. Guess the amount of butter by cutting it from a packet of known weight.

Beef Pie with Yoghurt

I have never been particularly interested in recipes for beef pies as the combination of meat and pastry does not appeal. In addition ready made pies available in shops and supermarkets take some beating so why bother. However when I saw this recipe it caught my eye as it is a beef pie which uses a cheese, potato and yoghurt topping so I tried it and liked it.

metric	*Ingredients*	*imperial*
450g	lean minced beef	1lb
2	bacon rashers	2
1	onion	1
1	garlic clove	1
1tbsp	tomato purée	1tbsp
400g	canned chopped tomatoes	14oz
1tsp	dried mixed herbs	1tsp
1	beef cube	1
675g	potatoes	1½ lb
300ml	natural yoghurt	10floz
2	eggs	2
75g	Cheddar cheese	3oz
1tbsp	vegetable oil	1tbsp

Method

Preheat the oven to 190°C. Prepare your ingredients first - peel and chop the onion and garlic, grate the cheese, cut the bacon into small pieces with a scissors and peel and slice the potatoes thinly. Place the beef, bacon, onion and garlic with oil in a pan and cook until the beef has browned. Stir in the tomato purée, chopped tomatoes, herbs and beef cube, bring to the boil and pour into a 24cm square 6cm deep (9 inch by 2½ inch) pie dish. Cook for 30 minutes in the oven. In the meantime boil the sliced potatoes in salted water for about 10 minutes by which time they should be soft but still firm. When the meat has finished cooking layer the potatoes over the top then beat together the yoghurt, cheese and the eggs and pour into the dish. Put back in the oven and cook for a further 25 minutes by which time the top should be brown.

Notes

If you are not too keen on beef try using minced lamb instead. The dimensions of the dish given above are only approximate - another way of looking at it is to use a 2 litre (3½ pint) dish.

Honey Roast Lamb

In my view, beef, lamb and pork have such distinctive tastes that they require very little enhancement and benefit very little from the introduction of other flavours. This is an exception - honey, rosemary and garlic add something extra to lamb which is very much to my taste. I remember eating lamb in a restaurant in Rome and while I do not have the recipe I am sure its superb taste owed a lot to garlic and rosemary. This dish is suitable for a Sunday lunch but it is particularly useful when you wish to provide guests with traditional fare but with a difference.

metric	**Ingredients**	*imperial*
2kg	leg of lamb	4½ lb
1tbsp	clear honey	1tbsp
1tsp	dried rosemary	1tsp
2	garlic cloves	2
4tbsp	vegetable oil	4tbsp

Method

Preheat the oven to 220°C. Place the lamb in a shallow roasting tin. Make five or six slits in the skin of the lamb using a sharp knife. Peel and slice the garlic into thin slivers and press into the slits in the lamb and pour over the honey spreading evenly with a knife. Sprinkle over the dried rosemary. Pour the oil into the bottom of the tin. Cook for about 30 minutes per 450g/1 pound, basting two or three times - the size of the joint in this recipe needs about two hours. When cooked cut into slices and serve with roast potatoes, parsnips and fried beans and onions.

Notes

Do not be concerned if the lamb begins to blacken as this is quite normal - if you think it is becoming too dark for your liking cover with aluminium foil. The recipe for the fried beans and onions can be found later in the book. To roast the potatoes and parsnips, peel, cut into pieces and place in the roasting tin with the meat about an hour before the lamb is due to finish cooking. Baste and turn the vegetables until they are browned all over.

Moussaka

When I lived on my own in London I ate out at a different restaurant almost every night. As a guide, I used a book which listed and described restaurants according to the quality of their food and value for money - decor was not considered so important. Not all lived up to their rating but one I liked and visited many times was a Greek restaurant in Soho. Unfortunately the entrance, via steps to a basement, was flanked on either side by sex shops so that when I recommended it to friends they took one look and decided to eat in Oxford Street where no doubt they paid twice the price for half the quality. One of my favourite dishes at this restaurant was moussaka with salad so I was keen to cook it myself but I had little success until I found the recipe below.

metric	*Ingredients*	*imperial*
1	*large aubergine*	*1*
2tbsp	*olive oil*	*2tbsp*
450g	*minced lamb*	*1lb*
1	*large onion*	*1*
700g	*potatoes*	*1½ lb*
230g	*chopped tomatoes canned*	*8oz*
1tsp	*sugar*	*1tsp*
1tsp	*dried mixed herbs*	*1tsp*
3	*tomatoes*	*3*
	salt	
	pepper	
50g	*butter*	*2oz*
50g	*flour*	*2oz*
625ml	*milk*	*1 pint*
50g	*Cheddar cheese*	*2oz*
2	*eggs*	*2*
	salt	
	pepper	

Method

Thinly slice the aubergine and arrange in layers in a colander, sprinkling salt liberally between them. Weigh down with a heavy plate and leave for an hour for the bitter juices to be drawn out. Wash under a tap and pat dry with a tea towel or kitchen tissue. Arrange the aubergine slices on a grill pan, brush with the oil then grill for about five minutes on each side. Brush with more oil when you turn them. Dry-fry the lamb in a large saucepan until brown. Chop the onions, add to the lamb and cook for a further five minutes then add the chopped tomatoes, sugar, herbs, and a pinch of salt and pepper. Bring to the boil, cover and simmer on low heat for 15 minutes. While waiting for the lamb to cook peel the potatoes and partly cook them (known as parboiling) for 10 minutes in salted water

- the time starts from the moment the water starts to boil. Pour half of the meat sauce into the bottom of a 2.25 litre (4 pint) ovenproof dish then place the aubergines and the fresh tomatoes (sliced) in layers over the top. Pour over the remaining meat sauce, then slice the potatoes and arrange to form another layer.

Turn on the oven to 180°C. then start making the cheese sauce. Grate the cheese on to a plate. Melt the butter in a saucepan, stir in the flour and cook for one minute on low heat. Remove the pan from the stove and gradually add the milk stirring well between each addition to remove lumps. Return the pan to the stove and bring the sauce to the boil stirring continuously until it thickens. Take off the stove and add the grated cheese then about half a teaspoon each of salt and pepper and stir until smooth. Finally separate the yolks from the egg whites, stir into the cheese sauce and pour over the top of the potatoes and cook in the oven for about 50-60 minutes when the top should be brown.

Notes

This recipe does seem rather complicated but try at least once to see if you like it and if it is worth the effort. I usually make it easy on myself by getting someone to make the cheese sauce as I am frying the meat etc. Moussaka goes well with a green salad.

Cartoon Cook Book... for Men

Lasagne

This recipe uses lasagne sheets which do not need precooking when used in dishes that are baked in the oven. The recipe is essentially that which I took from a standard cookery book but there are two important differences. Since beef stock is not something readily available in my kitchen I use a beef cube instead. More importantly I have introduced bacon which gives the dish extra flavour. The dish, bubbling and brown, when served with French bread and butter is an ideal centrepiece for a buffet style meal or as the main course of a more intimate dinner party.

metric	**Ingredients**	*imperial*
12 sheets	*lasagne*	*12 sheets*
450g	*minced beef lean*	*1lb*
4 rashers	*bacon*	*4 rashers*
1	*onion large*	*1*
400g	*tomatoes chopped canned*	*14oz*
4tbsp	*tomato purée*	*4tbsp*
1	*beef cube*	*1*
2tsp	*oregano*	*2tsp*
½ tsp	*salt*	*½ tsp*
½ tsp	*pepper*	*½ tsp*
1tbsp	*vegetable oil*	*1tbsp*
50g	*margarine*	*2oz*
50g	*flour*	*2oz*
50g	*Cheddar cheese*	*2oz*
25g	*Parmesan cheese*	*1oz*
½ tsp	*salt*	*½ tsp*
½ tsp	*pepper*	*½ tsp*
600ml	*milk*	*1pint*

Method

Chop the onion and fry in the oil in a large saucepan for about three minutes. Cut the bacon into small pieces using a scissors and discard the rind and any excess fat. Fry the bacon with the onions for a further three minutes, add the minced beef and continue frying until the meat is well browned. Add the tomatoes, tomato purée, oregano and half a teaspoon each of salt and pepper. Crumble in the beef cube and add 100ml (4floz) of hot water. Bring to the boil and simmer with the lid on for thirty minutes stirring occasionally.

Preheat the oven to 200°C. Grate the cheese on to a plate. Melt the margarine in a separate large saucepan, stir in the flour and cook for one minute on low heat. Remove the pan from the stove and add the milk gradually stirring well between each addition.

Return the pan to the heat and bring the sauce to the boil stirring continuously until it thickens. Take off the stove, add the grated cheese and half a teaspoon each of salt and pepper and stir until smooth.

Place half of the meat sauce in a 24cm (9 inch) square 6cm (2½ inch) deep oven proof dish (size is only approximate) and cover with six sheets of lasagne. If the surface is not completely covered adjust the number of sheets accordingly. Cover the pasta sheets with half of the cheese sauce. Repeat the layers of meat sauce, pasta and cheese. Sprinkle with grated Parmesan cheese and bake in the oven for 35 minutes.

Notes

Always get your ingredients ready before you start. For example, open the tin of tomatoes, measure out the tomato purée and milk, chop the onion and grate the cheese. The cheese sauce should be started about 15 minutes after the meat sauce has been set to simmer. At first you will think that the cheese sauce will never thicken so be patient. If you do not stand over it stirring as you wait it is sure to scorch. Use pregrated Parmesan which can be bought at a local store or supermarket.

Tagliatelle Carbonara

This dish is not one of my favourites as it does not have enough bite for me. My wife however really enjoys its rich creamy taste and I must admit it passes my good food test in that it leaves a very pleasant taste in the mouth. This recipe also has the virtue of being easy to prepare so try it and see what you think.

metric	**Ingredients**	*imperial*
300g	*tagliatelle*	*12oz*
50g	*cheddar cheese*	*2oz*
100g	*ham*	*4oz*
300ml	*half fat single cream*	*½ pint*
4	*eggs*	*4*
2	*garlic cloves*	*2*
1	*onion small*	*1*
1tbsp	*vegetable oil*	*1tbsp*
½ tsp	*salt*	*½ tsp*
½ tsp	*pepper*	*½ tsp*

Method

Cook the tagliatelle in plenty of boiling water to which has been added a pinch of salt in an uncovered saucepan until the pasta is soft to the bite. This usually takes about ten minutes. In the meantime peel the onion and garlic, chop finely and fry in the oil in a pan until soft. Grate the cheese and cut the ham into strips and put to one side. Beat the cream, eggs, salt and pepper together in a bowl then pour into the pan with the onions and heat gently until the mixture starts to thicken. Add the ham and cheese to the pan and stir until heated through. Drain the pasta in a sieve and add to the sauce in the pan mixing well. Serve immediately on heated plates.

Notes

This dish has a delicate flavour so make sure that the onion is small so that you do not use too much, otherwise the taste of the onion will predominate. The thin prepacked sheets of what I describe as "plastic" ham which you can buy at a supermarket are alright for this dish. Also of course any pasta can be used instead of tagliatelle.

Cannelloni

This dish requires a lot of patience as it uses tubes of pasta which have to be filled by hand. Since this is both fiddly and messy you may wonder why I have included the dish here - well, it is rather tasty and adds to your repertoire of Italian dishes.

metric	Ingredients	imperial
2tbsp	vegetable oil	2tbsp
1	onion large	1
2	garlic cloves	2
225g	lean minced beef	8oz
225g	frozen spinach	8oz
½ tsp	dried basil	½ tsp
½ tsp	dried oregano	½ tsp
¼ tsp	ground nutmeg	¼ tsp
1tsp	mixed herbs	1tsp
25g	butter	1oz
2	eggs	2
50g	grated parmesan	2oz
25g	cornflour	1oz
800g	canned chopped tomatoes	28oz
2tbsp	tomato purée	2tbsp
1tbsp	salt	1tsp
1tsp	pepper	1tsp
200g	cannelloni tubes	7oz

Method

Preheat the oven to 200°C. Peel and chop half the onion and one garlic clove and fry in the oil in a large saucepan for a few minutes until soft. Add the minced beef and heat until browned then pour into a large bowl. Cook the spinach in boiling water for a few minutes, sieve and add to the meat. Now sprinkle in the basil, oregano, nutmeg and half the salt and pepper and allow the mixture to cool. When cool stir in half the parmesan and the two eggs to make a smooth paste. Now comes the fiddly bit. Use your fingers to load the cannelloni tubes (usually there about 14 to 16) with the meat filling then arrange in a lightly greased dish approximately 24cm square by 6cm deep (9 inch square by 2½ inch deep).

Now to make the sauce. Chop the remaining onion and garlic, place in a bowl with the mixed herbs and microwave on full power for 3 minutes. Add the butter and microwave for a further minute until the butter has melted. Stir in the cornflour, chopped tomatoes, tomato purée and the remaining salt and pepper and continue mixing until smooth. Pour over the filled cannelloni tubes, sprinkle over remaining parmesan and cook in the oven for 30 minutes.

Cartoon Cook Book... for Men   *Cannelloni*

Notes

Be careful when filling the cannelloni tubes as they can fracture if handled roughly. To grease the baking dish use a small amount of vegetable oil. Use pregrated parmesan and cannelloni tubes that do not require precooking.

"Chicken   Cobbler"

Chilli Pasta

This dish is quick, simple and spicy. The relatively low fat combination of pasta and bacon is an attraction for those interested in healthy eating.

metric	*Ingredients*	*imperial*
300g	dried tagliatelle	12oz
6 rashers	bacon	6 rashers
1	onion medium size	1
400g	chopped tinned tomatoes	14oz
1tbsp	vegetable oil	1tbsp
½ tsp	chilli powder	½ tsp
1tbsp	tomato purée	1tbsp
1tsp	dried basil	1tsp
pinch	salt	pinch
pinch	pepper	pinch

Method

Chop the onion and heat in a saucepan with the oil until softened - it usually takes about five minutes. Cut the bacon into strips with scissors removing the fat according to taste. Add to the saucepan and fry for a further five minutes. Add the chilli powder, tomato purée, tomatoes, basil, salt, pepper and 150ml (¼ pint)of hot water. Bring to the boil and simmer for about 15 minutes.

In the meantime cook the pasta - place it in a saucepan, add a pinch of salt and cover it with water - put the lid on the saucepan, bring to the boil and simmer for about ten minutes. Sample a little piece of pasta - it is ready if it is soft to the bite. Sieve the pasta and place on warmed plates. Share the sauce between the plates and serve.

Notes

Other types of pasta such as penne will do equally well. Vary the amount of chilli powder according to taste. I once broke a tooth on a small piece of bone in a rasher of bacon so I am always watchful when cutting it up.

Polenta Pizza

I rarely eat pizzas in a British restaurant as I find their bases too thick and chewy, unlike in Italy where they are thin and crispy which is much more to my taste. Since a pizza is essentially a flat round base of dough with a topping of tomatoes and cheese they are not difficult to make. They are even easier if you buy ready made pizza bases in a supermarket and cover them with tinned tomatoes, grated cheese etc. before putting under a grill. If I want to make a quick pizza I usually use nan bread which can be bought at supermarkets and Indian stores - nan bread which contains coconut and dried fruit can make a very tasty pizza. If I am going to take the trouble of making a pizza from scratch I like to use a recipe which is a little different such as the one below.

metric	Ingredients	imperial
75g	plain flour	3oz
150g	polenta	6oz
2	eggs	2
1tsp	baking powder	1tsp
200ml	milk	6floz
100g	Cheddar cheese	4oz
400g	canned chopped tomatoes	14oz
1tsp	oregano	1tsp
1tsp	chopped herbs	1tsp
1tbsp	vegetable oil	1tbsp
1tsp	sugar	1tsp

Method

This recipe makes 2 large pizzas or 4 smaller ones. Put the milk and eggs in a bowl and beat together. Weigh out the flour and polenta, add the baking powder then sift into the eggs and milk. Stir to form a batter. Heat the oil in a frying pan and pour in some of the batter (half if you want two pizzas) and allow to spread thinly. Cook for about 5 minutes and when the top is set flip over using a fish slice and cook the other side also for about 5 minutes. Repeat for the second base adding more oil if necessary. Grate the cheese. Heat the the tomatoes and sugar in a saucepan or microwave oven then spread over the bases, add the cheese, sprinkle on the oregano and the mixed herbs before placing in a microwave or under a grill until the cheese has melted.

Notes

Polenta is ground from maize to form a type of flour which is used in Northern Italy as a staple food - it is used in some areas to make a bread which is dipped in milk and eaten for breakfast. The traditional way of making polenta is very time consuming but fortunately instant polenta can be bought at most supermarkets and delicatessen stores. Remember you can be adventurous - use almost anything you like to make your topping. The sugar is included in the recipe to remove the tartness of the canned tomatoes.

Cartoon Cook Book... for Men

Now for Goldfish Pie!

Tuna and Tomato Penne

My wife and I had this dish about once a week for a year until finally we tired of it. Before writing up these notes we tried it again and rekindled our taste for it - it is tasty, nutritious and exceptionally easy to prepare. If friends visit us at short notice and we are pushed to prepare a meal we often fall back on this recipe.

metric	Ingredients	imperial
350g	penne pasta	12oz
50g	anchovies canned	2oz
800g	chopped tomatoes canned	28oz
800g	ratatouille canned	28oz
½ tsp	black pepper	½ tsp
½ tsp	oregano	½ tsp
400g	tuna canned	14oz
2tbsp	parmesan cheese grated	2tbsp

Method

Cook the pasta in plenty of boiling water in a large saucepan to which about a teaspoon of salt has been added until a sample is soft to the bite - it usually takes about 10 minutes. Open all the cans and place the anchovies with their oil in a large saucepan and cut into small pieces with a knife and fork. Fry over a low heat for a few minutes. Add the tomatoes and ratatouille and season with the pepper and oregano and simmer for a few minutes. Drain the oil or water from the tuna and separate with a fork before adding to the saucepan. Drain the water from the pasta by tossing in a sieve and add to the hot sauce. Pour into a large serving dish, sprinkle with parmesan and place on the table for guests to help themselves.

Notes

I use ready grated parmesan bought from the supermarket. Since packets of dried pasta keep almost indefinitely and cans can be left in the cupboard until needed this is best described as a standby recipe. 800 grammes (28 ounces) of the tomatoes and ratatouille work out at two large cans each. Pasta comes in many shapes but for me penne tubes have the most appeal. Some shapes like pasta bows look silly whereas others like spaghetti while perhaps more typically Italian are more difficult to handle.

Salmon Pie

I think this recipe was given to me by relatives in Australia where it was called Pacific Pie and was based on tuna. It can be made with almost any fish but I prefer salmon. It is simple and quick to make and apart from the sweet potatoes uses ingredients found in most store cupboards.

metric	Ingredients	imperial
450g	potatoes	1lb
450g	sweet potatoes	1lb
200g	tinned salmon	7oz
50g	butter	2oz
25g	margarine	1oz
300ml	milk	½ pint
2tbsp	cornflour	2tbsp
1tsp	pepper	1tsp
1tsp	chopped dill	1tsp
1tsp	mustard	1tsp

Method

Peel and chop both types of potatoes to small chunks and boil in salted water for 20 minutes - the smaller you cut the potatoes the quicker they will cook. While the potatoes are cooking open the tin, drain and place the salmon in a pie dish about 1 litre (2 pints) in size. Without going to undue lengths remove the bones and skin and sprinkle over the dill. Now make a white sauce - melt the margarine in a saucepan over a low heat and stir in the cornflour to form a thick paste. Take the pan off the heat and slowly add the milk. Return the pan to the stove and bring to the boil stirring constantly until the mixture thickens. Stir in the mustard then pour the sauce over the salmon in the dish.

When the potatoes are soft, drain off the water then mash with most of the butter and add the pepper before spreading over the top of the salmon and the sauce. Finally chop the remaining butter and dot over the top of the pie before putting under a grill until the top is brown. Serve with salad.

Notes

If you cannot get sweet potatoes just use double the amount of the ordinary potatoes. Remember the quantities are not critical. For example the recipe lists 200 grammes of salmon but you may find the tin you buy contains 212 grammes. You can try this recipe with tuna or any other fish but be careful with the latter to remove any bones.

Fish and Chips

I really enjoy good quality fish and chips but it seems hardly worth while cooking them at home when you can buy the real thing at your local fish and chip shop. There is another good reason why I am somewhat reluctant to fry fish in the house - the smell can linger. Certainly if you are selling your house and are expecting potential purchasers just after lunch I can say from experience - forget fish, as their first impression of your home will be a fishy smell. However I am a lover of fish and will almost always order a fish course when I eat out and I do cook fish at home hence the recipe which follows. This recipe is worth noting just for the batter which can be used to coat for frying a variety of foods from vegetables to meat. I also enjoy chips in moderation although I do recognise that they have given British cooking a bad name - I know people who judge the quality of a restaurant by the amount of chips it serves with a meal. Why is it that French Fries are not looked down on in the same way as chips when they are essentially the same?

metric	*Ingredients*	*imperial*
4	*fish fillets*	*4*
1	*egg*	*1*
450ml	*milk*	*¾ pint*
175g	*plain flour*	*6oz*
100g	*cornflour*	*4oz*
½ tsp	*salt*	*½ tsp*
½ tsp	*caster sugar*	*½ tsp*
sachet	*easy-blend yeast*	*sachet*

Method

Sift the flour, cornflour, sugar and salt into a bowl and sprinkle in the yeast. Whisk the egg in a bowl with the milk which has been left to reach room temperature then slowly whisk into the flour mixture to form a smooth batter. Cover the top of the bowl and leave the batter for about two hours by which time it will increase in volume by about a half. Coat the fish fillets with flour then dip into the batter letting the excess drip off before deep frying for about five minutes in a basket in a large saucepan of hot vegetable oil. Place on kitchen tissue on a plate for a few minutes to let the excess fat drain before serving.

Notes

You can use a variety of fish to suit your taste but be aware of the bones. There are a number of ways you can do the chips - you can peel the potatoes and cut your own or buy ready cut for deep frying. To make it easy and avoid having to have two pans of boiling oil on top of the stove I usually use oven chips. Both the fish and the chips should be eaten as soon they are cooked so it is not a good idea to cook them in sequence.

FOR FULL SATISFACTION

Sometime ago I became ill with a stomach bug and completely lost my appetite - even pictures of food on television made me feel sick. When I recovered it was a great joy to feel hungry again but I would not have felt so good if I had not been able to satisfy my appetite. Many years earlier when all I knew about food was how to put it in my mouth I went to a French restaurant to celebrate a birthday and ordered chateaubriand the most expensive item on the menu. Thinking that the dish came with vegetables and garnish I declined to order anything else. Imagine my disappointment when I was served a piece of beef in the middle of an otherwise empty plate. Needless to say I went home feeling hungry and annoyed with myself. For full satisfaction most dishes need vegetables particularly potatoes, rice or pasta.

Vegetables are an essential part of most people's diet and are featured prominently in the traditional Sunday lunch in this country. Some critics say that British food is stodgy and unimaginative but traditional fare such as roast beef, Yorkshire pudding and vegetables (low calorie and fat free) is nourishing and tasty. Vegetables can be boiled, baked in their skins, roasted in the oven, shallow or deep fried, fried in batter, steamed or microwaved. Some vegetables such as parsnips are traditionally roasted alongside the Sunday joint until they are crisp and brown and many recipes can be found which use honey, chilli powder or other additives to give them that extra zing. Cooking instructions for the many vegetables which can be found at your local supermarket can be obtained from standard cookery books so I have contented myself by including here only those recipes for vegetables (and rice and pasta) which are of particular interest.

MENU - MAIN PLUS

Vegetables   **Page**

1   Fried Jacket Potatoes. 90
2   Caramelised Potatoes. 90
3   Garlic Potatoes. 90
4   Gratin Dauphinois. 91
5   Fried Beans and Onions. 92

Rice

1   Plain. 93
2   Sweet. 93

Pasta and Gnocchi. 94

Fried Jacket Potatoes

When I was young my mother used to cook potato fritters - thin slices of potato fried in a pan until brown. This is a quicker way of making them. Wash, then cook in their jackets in a microwave sufficient potatoes to suit your needs - one medium sized potato per person is usually enough. Allow to cool or if in a hurry plunge the potatoes in a bowl of cold water. When cool, slice the potatoes thinly. Heat some oil in a pan until quite hot then add about a teaspoon of mustard seeds which should start to pop. Fry the potato slices until they are brown. Some might think that this is very little different but cooking fritters takes ages whereas in this method there is no peeling, the microwave stage is simple and the frying takes only a few a minutes.

Caramelised Potatoes

Cook the potatoes in the microwave and slice as above but fry in the pan using one dessert spoon of vegetable oil, twenty five grammes (one ounce) of butter and one dessert spoon of brown sugar for every two medium sized potatoes.

Garlic Potatoes

Microwave the potatoes in their jackets and when cool cut in half. Scoop the centre out of each half potato and mix in a bowl with some chopped garlic (one clove between two potatoes), some chopped chives, salt, pepper and butter to taste. Fill the skins with the potato mixture, top with grated cheese and toast under a grill until the cheese melts.

Gratin Dauphinois

This is a very popular French dish which consists of sliced potatoes cooked in cream with a cheesy topping. It is rather rich for my taste but it can be a very impressive accompaniment to lamb and other meats. It is meant to be served in the dish in which it is cooked so that guests can help themselves.

metric	**Ingredients**	*imperial*
900g	*potatoes*	*2lb*
2	*garlic cloves*	*2*
50g	*butter*	*2oz*
150ml	*milk*	*¼ pint*
150ml	*single cream*	*¼ pint*
100g	*Cheddar cheese*	*4oz*
pinch	*salt*	*pinch*
pinch	*pepper*	*pinch*
pinch	*grated nutmeg*	*pinch*

Method

Preheat the oven to 200°C. Grease the inside of a medium sized shallow oven proof dish with a small amount of the butter. Peel and cut the potatoes into thin slices, dry on kitchen paper and lay them in overlapping lines in the dish. Peel and finely chop the garlic and sprinkle with the salt, pepper and nutmeg over the potatoes. Mix half the cream with the milk and pour in the dish. Grate the cheese and sprinkle evenly over the potatoes. Cut the butter into small pieces and dot over the potatoes before covering with aluminium foil and baking in the oven for 30 minutes. Then remove the foil and add the remaining cream slowly using a fork to disperse it among the potatoes. Bake for a further 20 minutes by which time the top should be brown and the potatoes tender.

Notes

This dish can be lightened by using plain yoghurt, Greek yoghurt or fromage frais instead of the cream to give a healthier alternative. It can also be used as a main course by putting other ingredients between the sliced potatoes such as sliced ham, chicken and mushrooms. The flavour can be varied by adding herbs and using different cheeses as topping.

Fried Beans and Onions

This dish goes particularly well with lamb and is a colourful and tasty change to the more conventional vegetables.

metric	Ingredients	imperial
225g	broad beans	8oz
1	onion medium sized	1
400	cannellini beans	14oz
1	red pepper	1
2tbsp	vegetable oil	2tbsp
2tbsp	sherry	2tbsp

Method

Cut the red pepper in half and remove the seeds, slice and fry in the oil in a large frying pan for about seven minutes. Peel and chop the onion into slivers, add to the pan and cook for a further three minutes by which time both the pepper and the onion should be soft. In the meantime cook the broad beans in boiling water for four to five minutes until soft to the bite. Sieve and add to the pan. Drain the liquid from the cannellini beans and put them in the pan with the sherry and simmer gently for about four minutes to warm through.

Notes

For this recipe I use frozen broad beans and a can of cannellini beans.

Plain Rice

For savoury and spicy dishes such as curries, basmati rice is preferred. Use about 75 grammes (3 ounces) per person. To cook put the rice in a suitably sized saucepan with a pinch of salt and cover completely with plenty of water. Bring to the boil, stir and lower the heat to simmer for about 10 to 15 minutes with the lid off when the water should be absorbed and a sample soft to the bite. Sieve and wash the rice in a colander with boiling water to remove the excess starch. Serve immediately or keep warm in a dish until needed. If the rice becomes cold it can be reheated in a microwave or by steaming in a colander on a saucepan containing boiling water.

Sweet Rice

An Asian friend gave me this recipe - her family eat it as a dessert but my wife and I like it so much that we serve it with a curry or satay instead of plain rice. I have never seen this type of rice dish available in an Asian restaurant and can only assume that it is because sweet rice takes a little more time to prepare. If you like sweet things this will please you.

metric	*Ingredients*	*imperial*
450g	*basmati rice*	*1lb*
225g	*sugar*	*8oz*
25g	*butter*	*1oz*
pinch	*food colour egg yellow*	*pinch*
4tbsp	*raisins*	*4tbsp*

Method

Soak the rice for at least an hour in cold water to remove the starch. In a separate saucepan bring to the boil one and a quarter pints (750ml) of water to which you add the colouring - by experience you can vary the amount to get the colour you prefer. Sieve the rice and add to the boiling water and cook for ten minutes or until the rice is soft to the bite. Sieve the rice which is now coloured using a colander and put to one side. In a separate saucepan melt the butter, take off the heat and add the sugar and about 100ml (4floz) of water. Slowly bring to the boil stirring constantly until the mixture becomes tacky when sampled with a spoon. Add the rice to the pan and mix so that it is coated with the sugary liquid and continue to heat until almost dry. Add the raisins and serve.

Notes

The colouring for the rice can be bought at Asian stores. Add more or less depending on the depth of colour which is pleasing to your eye. The colouring can be left out if you prefer but the deep orange/yellow colour can look strikingly effective when the rice is put on on the table. The amounts specified in the recipe are enough for four to six people but I rarely cook less as any left over can be put in the freezer for use on another occasion. When entertaining guests serve plain rice as well so that they can mix the two to suit their taste.

Pasta

Pasta is made from durum wheat which has a high gluten content and is to Italians what potatoes are to the British - the filling part of the meal which carries the flavours from the meat and sauces. Pasta comes in a variety of shapes from the simple to the elaborate such as bows and shells - it can be cooked easily in boiling water for about ten minutes. Some cooks put oil in the water to prevent the pasta from sticking but there is no need to do this if you stir often at the start. The pasta is ready when a sample is soft but firm to the bite.

Gnocchi

Gnocchi which are little dumplings made from potato and flour are usually eaten by Italians as a first course sprinkled with butter and Parmesan cheese or coated with a rich spicy tomato sauce. On their own gnocchi can be rather bland but can be flavoured with spinach, chilli powder etc.

metric	*Ingredients*	*imperial*
900g	*potatoes*	*2lb*
225g	*self raising flour*	*8oz*
1	*egg*	*1*
pinch	*salt*	*pinch*
pinch	*pepper*	*pinch*
pinch	*grated nutmeg*	*pinch*

Method

Peel the potatoes, cut them into chunks and boil in plenty of salted water for about 20 minutes or microwave whole for about 10-15 minutes depending on power then peel off the skin. If boiled, pour the potatoes into a colander while warm so they dry off as quickly as possible. Mash thoroughly in a saucepan adding the salt, pepper and nutmeg. Beat in the flour to form a soft smooth dough which is easy to work. Roll out the dough on a floured surface to form a long sausage about 2cm (³/₄ inch) in diameter. Cut into 2cm (³/₄ inch) lengths and score each with a fork to produce a ribbed effect. Bring a large pan of salted water to the boil then let it simmer. Drop in as many gnocchi as you can - they are done when they float to the surface which usually takes about 2-3 minutes. Scoop them out, drain and transfer to a preheated oven proof dish and keep warm until served.

Cartoon Cook Book... for Men

Honeymoon and Other Salads

Lettuce alone has been described rather humorously as honeymoon salad but there are many salads with much more interesting ingredients. Almost anything can be put in salads - tomatoes, cucumber, onions, apples, melon, kiwi fruit, nuts and raisins to name just a few. When making a salad just use your imagination and choose what you like - do not be bound by convention. For example I do not like iceberg lettuce and would not include it in a salad as although popular it seems more like cabbage to me - I prefer the more delicate flavour of the greener British grown variety.

Salads can be served as a tasty stylish first course or as a main course. In the former vegetables, fruit and eggs would predominate whereas in the latter one would find more filling ingredients such as cheese, meat, poultry and pasta. You will know what you like in salads so to provide a list of recipes would serve no purpose. However you may not know how to make dressings which enhance the flavour and add that touch of piquancy which makes all the difference. Accordingly I have listed recipes for some of the most popular salad dressings. "Salad cream" is the commercially marketed version of mayonnaise which some will say is as different to a good dressing as chalk is to cheese. My advice is to try these dressings but if you do not like them stick to your salad cream - after all manufacturers have invested vast sums of money getting it right for you.

"Tossed Salad"

Vinaigrette

olive oil	175ml (6floz)
cider vinegar	2tbsp
lemon juice	2tbsp
sugar	1tsp
garlic clove	1
mixed herbs	2tbsp

Crush the garlic and place in a bowl with all the other ingredients. Add a pinch of salt and pepper and whisk together with a fork. This is perhaps the most popular of all salad dressings - some versions contain mustard or Worcester sauce for extra flavour.

Yoghurt and Mint

natural yoghurt	300ml (½ pint)
mint jelly	150g (6oz)
sugar	1tsp

This is very easy to make, simply whisk the mint jelly into the yoghurt with a fork and add the sugar to taste. This dressing goes well with Indian food and is usually served with onion bhajias.

Honey and Mint

clear honey	2tbsp
cider vinegar	4tbsp
olive oil	3tbsp
chopped mint	1tbsp

Whisk the ingredients together in a bowl with a fork adding salt and pepper to taste.

Mayonnaise

egg yolk	1
salt	¼ tsp
pepper	¼ tsp
mustard powder	¼ tsp
olive oil	150ml (¼ pint)
tarragon vinegar	½ tbsp

Whisk the egg yolk and seasoning in a bowl and add the oil drop by drop until the mixture thickens, then stir in the vinegar. If the mayonnaise becomes too thick it can be thinned with a small amount of water. You should note that this recipe uses uncooked eggs. Vulnerable people such as the elderly, the sick, babies and pregnant women are advised not to eat raw eggs or uncooked food made from them because of the risk of salmonella poisoning. However it is generally accepted that for healthy people the risk is small.

"Boiled Egg"

IF YOU MUST

Some people find making pastry a pleasant relaxing experience but I am not one of them. I usually end up with bits of pastry sticking to my fingers from where it seems to travel all over the kitchen - on taps, door handles and floor. This is why I prefer to buy ready made pastry from a supermarket and recommend that you do the same. However if you have an overwhelming urge and must make pastry or you do not live near a convenient source of supply these notes are for you.

Shortcrust Pastry

Since there is no such thing as longcrust pastry and even standard cookery books do not explain what the pastry is short of, the origin of the name is not too clear. Most books will tell you that shortcrust refers to a crumbly pastry which is used to make apple pies etc. A standard recipe is -

metric	Ingredients	imperial
100g	plain flour	4oz
25g	margarine	1oz
25g	lard	1oz
pinch	salt	pinch

Sieve the flour and salt into a large bowl. Add the fats cut into small pieces and rub into the flour with the fingers. When the mixture resembles bread crumbs add cold water a little at a time until you have a smooth ball of dough which will leave the bowl clean. It is important to keep the pastry cool so work quickly. Leaving the pastry in a polythene bag in a fridge for about 20 minutes before using also helps to prevent it breaking when rolled. Baking takes about 15 minutes in an oven preheated to 230°C.

Puff Pastry

Be warned this is even more difficult to make. It is the pastry used for sausage rolls, vol-au-vents etc. which when cooked consists of a number of thin layers - in French, millefeuille, a thousand layers. This is achieved by layering the fat in the flour rather rubbing it in. One recipe is -

metric	*Ingredients*	*imperial*
225g	*plain flour*	*8oz*
100g	*margarine*	*4oz*
100g	*lard*	*4oz*
250ml	*iced water*	*5floz*
½ tsp	*lemon juice*	*½ tsp*

Sieve the flour and salt into a large bowl then add the fat cut into small pieces. Mix gently to coat the fat but do not rub in. Make a well in the centre of the mixture then pour in the water and lemon juice. Draw a knife through the mixture in all directions so that all the water blends in. Gently mould the mixture into a slab and roll out. By overlapping and rolling a number of times try and trap as much air as possible between the layers. Wrap the pastry in polythene and chill in a fridge for as long as possible preferably overnight. Allow to cool to room temperature before rolling then bake in a preheated oven for about 15 minutes at 230°C or higher.

Baking Blind

This does not mean baking when you have had too much to drink but means baking the pastry base separately from the other ingredients which make up the pie. This is necessary when you want to make a free standing flan or when the topping such as a meringue would burn long before the pastry has cooked. When baking blind it important to remove any air from under the pastry otherwise it will bubble up on cooking. Some books recommend adding beads on foil to weigh down the pastry but a simpler way is to prick the pastry to allow the air to escape. When not baking blind always put the dish on a metal tray in the oven so that the heat is conducted efficiently and the base under the filling cooks thoroughly. Also rather than baking blind to help prevent the bases of tarts being soggy try brushing them with egg white before baking.

Cartoon Cook Book... for Men

SWEET THINGS

Most men like sweet things and will happily forego the rest of the meal for a number of helpings of desserts. Unfortunately the fashion for making food look pretty at the expense of taste extends even to sweets with restaurants moving away from traditional British desserts such as hearty helpings of apple pie and custard to mini servings of continental style dishes. How often are we confronted when dining out today, by pretentious desserts which look colourful on the plate but which can be devoured in one mouthful?

As a change from the Sunday roast I often take my wife to a charming little fish restaurant overlooking the bay near our home - since the restaurant is a fish and chip shop on the promenade of a popular seaside resort, the description above is pretentious or in other words I am showing off!! My advice is to make your food look as attractive as possible for guests but avoid ostentation and go more for taste rather than visual appeal with your sweets as well as the rest of your cooking. Serve desserts which are good to eat in preference to ones that you think might impress your friends.

There is a large variety of sweets for you to choose - from the light and fanciful to the hearty and substantial. Your choice from the selection which follows must be dictated by what you and your guests like and what has gone before in the meal. For example after a heavy starter or main course a bowl of fruit on your table can be a most attractive and effective way of rounding off a meal. It will have particular appeal for those who have overindulged on the earlier courses and those unfortunates who cannot sit down to a meal without worrying about calories and cholesterol.

MENU - DESSERTS

Pies and Pastry   Page

1. Pecan Pie. 103
2. Toffee Apple Pie. 104
3. Apple Strudel. 105
4. Custard Apple Pie. 107
5. American Apple Pie. 109
6. Lemon Cheesecake. 110
7. Custard Tart. 113
8. Lemon Meringue Pie. 114
9. Mississippi Mud Pie. 115
10. Quick Coconut Pie. 116

Puddings

1. Macaroni. 117
2. Christmas. 118
3. Blackberry Batter. 121
4. Whisky Rice. 122
5. Exotic Bread and Butter. 123

Others

1. Apple Crisp. 124
2. Ginger Soufflé. 125
3. Pancakes. 126
4. Banana and Coconut Fritters. 128
5. Tiramisu. 129
6. Home-made Ice Cream. 130
7. Orange Creams. 131
8. Lemon Syllabub. 132
9. Simple Sherry Trifle. 133
10. Pears in Wine. 134

Pecan Pie

I was given two recipes for pecan pie - one from friends in North Carolina U.S.A. which I must accept as an authentic version of this popular American dessert - the other from a British source which used golden instead of maple syrup. Unfortunately neither recipe worked well for me - one pie was runny when baked whereas the other was too stiff and dry. By trial and error I arrived at the recipe below which works every time and produces a pie which is delicious warm or cold with cream or ice cream. This is one of my most popular desserts.

metric	*Ingredients*	*imperial*
250g	*shortcrust pastry frozen*	*9oz*
100g	*brown sugar*	*4oz*
2	*eggs*	*2*
½ tsp	*vanilla essence*	*½ tsp*
40g	*butter*	*1½ oz*
1tbsp	*golden syrup*	*1tbsp*
2tbsp	*maple syrup*	*2tbsp*
100g	*pecan nuts*	*4oz*

Method

Take the pastry out of the freezer and leave to defrost for a few hours. Preheat the oven to 180°C. Roll out the pastry on a floured pastry board or clean worktop and line a 20cm wide 4cm deep (8 inches by 1½ inches) greased pie dish. Melt the butter in a bowl, add the eggs and beat together. Beat in the sugar, vanilla essence and the golden and maple syrups until the mixture is smooth and free from lumps. Pour into the lined dish and float the pecan nuts on top with the flatter sides up as though they were little boats. Fill in any small uncovered areas with broken pieces of nuts. Any nuts over can be saved for another time. Bake for 30 minutes when the pie should have risen to fill the dish.

Notes

The recipe works quite well with maple syrup substitute. To melt the butter, place in a dish in a microwave on low power for a few minutes or in an oven or warm water. To grease the pie dish coat the inside with a small amount of butter or vegetable oil. When golden syrup is thick it is difficult to measure - to make it thinner place the jar with the lid off in a microwave for about 30 seconds. Using ready made pastry reduces the work enormously but if you prefer to make your own, good luck to you.

Toffee Apple Pie

You will see that this recipe is very similar to that for pecan pie except that apples are used instead of nuts. The cornflour and the longer cooking time are necessary to gel the syrup mixture which can be inhibited by the presence of the apples. I prefer to use dessert apples such as Cox which I core but do not bother to peel. For a less sweet version use cooking apples. For convenience the recipe is repeated in full.

metric	Ingredients	imperial
250g	shortcrust pastry frozen	9oz
100g	brown sugar	4oz
2	eggs	2
½ tsp	vanilla essence	½ tsp
40g	butter	1½ oz
1tbsp	golden syrup	1tbsp
2tbsp	maple syrup	2tbsp
1tbsp	cornflour	1tbsp
2	apples	2

Method

Preheat the oven to 180°C. Roll out the defrosted pastry on a floured pastry board or cleaned worktop and use it to line a 20cm wide 4cm deep (8 inches by 1½ inches) greased pie dish. Melt the butter in a bowl add the eggs and beat together with the sugar, vanilla essence and the golden and maple syrups until the mixture is lump free.

Remove the cores from the apples, slice thinly and place neatly in layers in the lined dish. Stir the cornflour into a tablespoon of cold water and add to the syrup mixture before pouring over the apples. Any pastry over can be used to decorate the pie as you wish. Bake in the oven for 40 minutes when the mixture should be set and the pastry cooked.

Notes

Do not mess about trying to remove the apple cores with a knife unless you have to - buy a specially designed corer from a kitchen utensil shop. If you use a microwave oven to melt the butter remember that metal objects such as knives, jar lids etc. should never be put in with it.

Apple Strudel

In its original form this recipe was a disaster. It required laying sheets of filo pastry on a towel, brushing with molten butter, spreading the apple mixture over the pastry and rolling into a Swiss type roll. Unfortunately, following the instructions to the letter produced a roll about 36cm (14 inches) long and 14cm (6 inches) wide which defied all my attempts to wrestle it on to a baking tray in one piece. It broke apart and even when I got the pieces into the oven the pastry became too brittle when baked. It was apparent that the ingredients were about four times too much, the apple needed to be chopped very finely and something had to be added to absorb the excess moisture which came from the apples. This recipe, which evolved from trial and error should not give you any problems. The filo pastry is replaced by puff pastry which can be bought at supermarkets ready made and is much easier to work with and bread crumbs are added to absorb the moisture.

metric	*Ingredients*	*imperial*
250g	*puff pastry frozen*	*9oz*
50g	*sugar*	*2oz*
1	*dessert apple large*	*1*
25g	*butter*	*1oz*
25g	*almonds flaked*	*1oz*
25g	*raisins*	*1oz*
7tbsp	*bread crumbs*	*7tbsp*
1tsp	*ground cinnamon*	*1tsp*
¼ tsp	*nutmeg powder*	*¼ tsp*
¼ tsp	*vanilla essence*	*¼ tsp*
1tbsp	*icing sugar*	*1tbsp*
pinch	*salt*	*pinch*

Method

Take the pastry out of the freezer and leave to defrost for a few hours. Preheat the oven to 200°C. Melt the butter in a saucepan on a stove or in a bowl in a microwave oven. Core and chop the apple very small and add to the butter with the nuts, raisins, salt, sugar, cinnamon, nutmeg, vanilla essence and bread crumbs. Roll out the pastry on a floured pastry board or clean worktop until it is approximately 30cm by 20cm (12 inches by 8 inches). Trim the edges by using the rolling pin as a straight rule until a rectangle is obtained. Spread the apple mixture evenly over the pastry leaving about 3cm (1 inch) clear at one of the shorter sides of the rectangle. Pat the mixture flat so that no sharp apple pieces can protrude into the pastry and carefully roll up towards the clear edge. Brush the clear edge with milk to help seal it and turn the strudel over so the join is underneath. If some of the mixture falls out at the ends push it back in with your fingers Brush the inside of the ends with milk and fold in as though you were packing a parcel. Plunge a fork into the strudel twice at equal distances to allow it to breathe and brush all

Apple Strudel Cartoon Cook Book... for Men

over with milk. Place in a greased baking tray and cook for thirty minutes. When cooked sieve over the icing sugar and serve hot or cold with cream or ice cream.

Notes

Bread crumbs can be bought ready prepared in a store or supermarket. One round of bread can be used to produce the required amount of crumbs - the easiest way to crumb the bread is to break it into small pieces and place in a blender for a few minutes but you can also use a cheese grater. Cox apples are ideal for this dish but if you like a sharper taste use cooking apples and add more sugar.

"Pork Chop"

Custard Apple Pie

This is the Rolls-Royce of apple pies - the custard gives a luxurious taste which lingers in the mouth. The original recipe used filo pastry but this is not easy to use and requires brushing with too much butter for my liking so I recommend ready made puff pastry instead. Although an advocate of the use of canned products whenever possible the rich taste of freshly made custard justifies the extra effort involved in this recipe.

metric	**Ingredients**	*imperial*
250g	frozen puff pastry defrosted	9oz
3	dessert apples medium size	3
2tbsp	raisins	2tbsp
3	eggs	3
110g	caster sugar	4oz
1½ tbsp	plain flour	1½ tbsp
1tbsp	cornflour	1tbsp
1tsp	vanilla essence	1tsp
300ml	milk	½ pint

Method

Preheat the oven to 210°C. Grease a pie dish sized approximately 20cm (8 inch) long 4cm (1½ inch) deep with butter or vegetable oil. Divide the pastry into two halves. Roll out one half on a floured pastry board or clean worktop and line the dish. Peel, core and slice the apples and stew in boiling water in a saucepan to which a table spoon of sugar has been added for 15 minutes - this sugar is ordinary sugar additional to that specified in the recipe. Remove the pan from the heat, drain, then spread the apples evenly over the pastry in the bottom of the dish. Spread the raisins evenly over the apples and press down gently with a fork.

Pour the milk into a saucepan and heat until almost boiling. Separate the egg yolks from the whites by breaking each egg against the side of a bowl and with the long axis vertical allow the white to fall into a dish. Keep pouring the yolk from half eggshell to half eggshell until all the white has separated. Put the yolks into a large bowl - the whites can be discarded. Add the caster sugar to the yolks and beat together until smooth and creamy. Gradually sieve in the flour and cornflour. Now whisk in the warm milk a little at a time with a fork then finally add the vanilla essence. Pour the mixture into a saucepan and bring to the boil stirring constantly. Reduce the heat and continue stirring until the custard thickens. Cover the apples in the pie dish with the custard as evenly as possible and allow it to cool for about five minutes. Roll out the remaining pastry and use it to cover the top of the pie. A little milk brushed along the edge of the pastry in the dish before covering will help to give a good seal. Press down the top and covering pastry at the edge with a fork to effect the seal. Plunge a knife twice into the pie to enable it to breathe. Brush the pie with milk and bake in the oven for thirty minutes by which time

Custard Apple Pie

it should be golden brown. When cool you can if you wish sieve over a fine layer of icing sugar for decoration.

Notes

Cox apples are ideal for this recipe. Serve the pie with cream or ice cream but even on its own it tastes delicious.

"Scrambled Egg"

American Apple Pie

If you like thick crunchy apple pie with a taste of cinnamon this recipe is for you. When served "a la mode", as the Americans say, with ice cream it is delicious.

metric	*Ingredients*	*imperial*
250g	*shortcrust pastry frozen*	*9oz*
75g	*caster sugar*	*3oz*
170g	*evaporated milk*	*3oz*
3	*dessert apples medium*	*3*
2tbsp	*cornflour*	*2tbsp*
1tsp	*cinnamon*	*1tsp*

Method

Defrost the pastry for a few hours before using. Preheat the oven to 190°C. Grease a 20cm wide by 4cm deep (8inch by 1½ inch) pie dish with a small amount of butter or vegetable oil. Peel, core and chop the apples to about peanut size. Divide the pastry into two and roll out one half on a floured pastry board or cleaned worktop and use to line the bottom and sides of the dish. Sift together the caster sugar, cornflour and cinnamon into a bowl and add the evaporated milk a little at a time mixing thoroughly. Spread the apple over the bottom of the dish and pour over the mixture. Press the apple down gently until it is level. Roll out the remaining pastry to cover the dish but before doing so brush the edges of the pastry in the dish with milk to help seal the two layers. Brush the top of the pie with milk. Make 4 vent holes in the top of the pie with a knife and bake in the oven for 40 minutes by which time the pastry should be brown.

Notes

Any dessert apples will do but Cox are ideal. Since the apple is not precooked the pie should be thick and crunchy. Make sure that the pie dish is deep enough to take the apples - remember that the size specified is only a guide. To decorate the top of the pie you can sieve over a fine layer of icing sugar if you wish. Place the dish on a tray just in case you have over filled it and the juices from the pie boil over in the oven. Use a fork to press down the edges of the pastry to help seal the two layers.

Lemon Cheesecake

I tried a number of recipes for cheesecake before I found this one but none were completely satisfactory - mostly they used ground digestive biscuits mixed with butter to form the base and while the results were acceptable they were too sweet and cloying for my taste. This recipe produces a top quality cheesecake and is worth the extra work involved. When I tell you that the first time I tried to make this dessert it was a disaster hopefully you will realise that we can all make mistakes. You will see that the recipe uses a 23cm (9inch) cake tin but carelessly I picked a much smaller one and soon began to panic when I realised that I would not be able to get all the filling in the tin. Would you believe I actually slit the base which I had already baked, along its length and using a second tin made two cheesecakes! Since both tasted delicious I got away with it but if that ever happens again I think I will put the surplus in the freezer to use another day.

metric	*Ingredients*	*imperial*
	for the base	
75g	*butter*	*3oz*
75g	*caster sugar*	*3oz*
1	*egg*	*1*
2tbsp	*milk*	*2tbsp*
75g	*self raising flour*	*3oz*
1½ tsp	*baking powder*	*1½ tsp*
1tsp	*ground cinnamon*	*1tsp*
	for the filling	
450g	*low fat cream cheese*	*1lb*
200g	*low fat fromage frais*	*7oz*
4	*eggs*	*4*
225g	*caster sugar*	*8oz*
4tbsp	*lemon juice*	*4tbsp*
25g	*plain flour*	*1oz*
25g	*flaked almonds*	*1oz*
75g	*sultanas*	*3oz*

Method

Preheat the oven to 160°C. Grease a 23cm (9 inch) spring-clipped cake tin with vegetable oil on a piece of paper towel. Mix together the butter and caster sugar then add the egg and the milk. Sieve over the flour, baking powder and cinnamon. Mix well and spoon into the prepared tin spreading evenly to cover the base. Bake for 30 minutes. The next stage is to prepare the filling. Separate the yolks from the whites of the eggs. Put the cheese, fromage frais, egg yolks, caster sugar and lemon juice into a large bowl and beat until the mixture is smooth and creamy. This can be hard work so use a big spoon or try an electric whisk. Sieve over the plain flour and stir in gently before mixing the almonds and sultanas as evenly as possible through the mixture. Now whisk the egg whites until they just begin to peak - then gently stir into the cheese mixture so that as much air as possible is retained in the egg whites. Pour the mixture over the cooked base and level off the top. Bake in the oven for one hour but when the top begins to brown usually after about 20 minutes cover with aluminium foil. When the hour has passed switch off the oven but leave the cheesecake inside to cool slowly to prevent sinking in the middle.

Notes

This cheesecake is best served chilled with cream or ice cream. In view of this and the fact that the cheesecake is allowed to cool in the oven to keep sinkage to a minimum it is best cooked the night before you plan to use it. It is not essential to use a spring-clipped cake tin but it is so much easier to remove the cheesecake from it.

Cartoon Cook Book... for Men

Custard Tart

When I was a young boy a custard tart bought at the local cake shop was a much enjoyed tea time treat so I thought it would be nice to make my own. Looking through my cook books I was bewildered by the variation in the recipes - some used milk others cream while some used flour others did not. Finally after trying many recipes which did not work I found the recipe below which works well for me every time. I trust it will be the same for you.

metric	Ingredients	imperial
250g	frozen shortcrust pastry defrosted	9oz
3	eggs	3
110g	caster sugar	4oz
1½ tbsp	plain flour	1½ tbsp
1 tbsp	cornflour	1 tbsp
1 tsp	vanilla essence	1 tsp
300ml	milk	½ pint

Method

Preheat the oven to 190°C. Roll out the pastry on a floured pastry board or cleaned worktop and use it to line a 20cm wide 4cm deep (8 by 1½ inches) lightly greased pie dish. Prick the pastry with a fork, brush with some of the milk and place in the oven for 20 minutes. Pour the milk into a saucepan and heat slowly until almost boiling. Separate the yolks from the whites and put them into a large mixing bowl - the whites can be discarded or kept in the fridge to use at a later date. Beat together the egg yolks and sugar until smooth and creamy. Gradually sieve in the flour and cornflour and beat until smooth. Whisk in the warm milk a little at a time with a fork and add the vanilla essence. Pour the mixture into a saucepan and bring to the boil stirring constantly. Reduce the heat and continue stirring until the custard thickens. Pour into the pastry case and bake for a further 10 minutes. To appreciate the flavour it is best to eat it hot or cold on its own but there is nothing to stop you adding cream or ice cream if you wish.

Notes

The custard will thicken from the bottom of the saucepan so make sure you prevent it building up by constant stirring. It is also preferable to put it in the pastry case when it is still pourable but if the custard becomes jelly like use a wet knife to spread it evenly in the pastry case. Traditionally egg custards are dusted with a fine layer of ground cinnamon and icing sugar - to do this use a sieve.

Lemon Meringue Pie

This is an old favourite which is easy to make and if you like the sharp taste of lemon it is a dessert which will feature high on your list. The recipe below is a combination of two - one I found in a standard cookery book the other in a magazine. I tried both recipes a number of times but was not happy until by combining parts of each I arrived at what I thought was a really tasty result. See what you think.

metric	**Ingredients**	*imperial*
250g	shortcrust pastry frozen	*9oz*
2	lemons	*2*
1tbsp heaped	cornflour	*heaped 1tbsp*
200g	caster sugar	*8oz*
2	eggs	*2*

Method

Take the pastry out of the freezer and leave to defrost for a few hours. Preheat the oven to 200°C. Lightly grease the inside of a 20cm wide by 4cm deep (8 inch by 1½ inch) pie dish with a small amount of butter or vegetable oil. Roll out the pastry on to a floured pastry board or clean worktop and line the dish. Press the pastry down firmly to remove any trapped air then prick over a few times with a fork. Bake in the oven for 15 minutes. In the meantime rub the lemons against a grater to shred the peel and put to one side. Cut the bald lemons in half and squeeze hard over a sieve on top of a measuring jug to collect the juice which is then made up to 300ml (½ pint) with water. Now separate the egg whites from the yolks In a pan, mix together the lemon juice, peel, cornflour and half the sugar. Bring to the boil on low heat stirring all the time until the mixture thickens. Remove from the heat and stir in the egg yolks. Pour the mixture into the cooked pie case.

Now to make the meringue - whisk together the egg whites in a bowl until they begin to form peaks when the whisk is withdrawn. Then slowly add the rest of the sugar in a slow steady stream whisking all the time. The meringue should now resemble thick cream. Spoon the meringue over the lemon filling. Reduce the temperature of the oven to 180°C. Bake the pie for 15 minutes when the top should be brown and crisp.

Notes

I prefer eating this dessert slightly warm with ice cream but it also goes well with cream. If you get some of egg yolk mixed in with the whites you will find that they will not whisk well. This a good example of the need to bake the pastry separately (known as baking blind) - otherwise the meringue would burn well before the pastry is cooked. I would not try to make the meringue by hand - you really need an electric whisk to do the job properly.

Mississippi Mud Pie

Some people say that it is difficult to eat well in America at a reasonable cost whereas others are delighted with both the quality and quantity of the food they find on their American holidays. To eat or rather dine out to the standard found in good restaurants in Europe can cost an arm and a leg but there can be no doubt that some of the fast food chain restaurants provide value and quality which take some beating. One chain is much to my liking and it is at one of their restaurants that I first tried Mississippi mud pie. I liked the rich chocolate taste of this dessert very much so that when I came across the recipe I was keen to try it. Much to my surprise the recipe with only a few slight modifications worked well first time so if you like chocolate put this one at the top of your list to try. The name apparently comes from the fact that the pie is of a colour similar to that of Mississippi mud.

metric	**Ingredients**	*imperial*
250g	*frozen shortcrust pastry*	*9oz*
100g	*plain chocolate*	*4oz*
50g	*butter*	*2oz*
3tbsp	*golden syrup*	*3tbsp*
3	*eggs*	*3*
150g	*caster sugar*	*5oz*
1tsp	*vanilla essence*	*1tsp*
140g	*whipping cream*	*5floz*
1tbsp	*cocoa powder*	*1tbsp*

Method

Take the pastry out of the freezer and allow to come up to room temperature. Preheat the oven to 200°C. Roll out the pastry on a floured pastry board or clean worktop and line a 20cm wide 4cm deep (8inches by 1½ inches) greased pie dish. Pierce the pastry with a fork a few times and bake in the oven for about 15 minutes by which time it should start to brown. Melt the chocolate and butter with the syrup in a microwave or by placing the bowl in hot water. Allow to cool for a few minutes then stir in the beaten eggs, sugar and vanilla essence. Pour the chocolate mixture into the baked pastry mould and cook in the oven for about 40 minutes when the filling should have set firm. Leave to cool completely. To serve, whip the cream until it peaks when the whisk is removed and spread over the chocolate filling. Finally sieve the cocoa evenly over the cream.

Notes

To grease the pie dish coat the inside with a small amount of butter or vegetable oil on a piece of kitchen paper. Thin the golden syrup by placing the jar with the lid off in a microwave for about 30 seconds so that it can be measured more easily. You can serve this pie with cream or ice cream but it is quite rich and goes down well on its own. To whisk the cream you will need an electric whisk. If you do not have plain try milk chocolate adding about twenty percent more.

Quick Coconut Pie

This dessert is remarkably simple and quick. If you like coconut this is for you. The pie when cooked has a rather cake like consistency and is delicious with cream or ice cream.

metric	Ingredients	imperial
50g	butter	2oz
100g	caster sugar	4oz
2	eggs	2
100g	desiccated coconut	4oz
50g	plain flour	2oz
½ tsp	ground nutmeg	½ tsp
½ tsp	vanilla essence	½ tsp
150ml	milk	¼ pint

Method

Preheat the oven to 180°C. Lightly grease a one litre (1¾ pint) pie dish. Whisk together or liquidise in a blender all the ingredients until smooth. Pour into the dish and bake for 45 minutes by which time the top should be firm and golden brown.

Notes

Chop the butter in to small pieces before adding to the mixture as above. However I find it easier to melt the butter first in a microwave or in a bowl of hot water. If you do this add the butter last to the other mixed ingredients.

Macaroni Pudding

When I was a boy the staple sweets at home were apple pie, rice pudding and macaroni pudding. Recipes for apple pie can be found in almost every cookery book and some for rice pudding crop up occasionally but macaroni pudding seems to have disappeared without trace. On one occasion I spent a very frustrating afternoon searching through all the cookery books in my local library but could not find one recipe. This is strange when you think how popular pasta has become particularly with the health crowd. With pleasant memories of macaroni puddings I made up a recipe myself which gave me a good result first time.

metric	*Ingredients*	*imperial*
175g	*macaroni*	*6oz*
600ml	*milk*	*1 pint*
2tbsp	*single cream*	*2tbsp*
75g	*sugar*	*3oz*
10g	*butter*	*½ oz*
pinch	*ground nutmeg*	*pinch*

Method

Preheat the oven to 200°C. Place the macaroni in a one litre (1¾ pint) pie dish. Add the sugar and cream and pour on the milk. Float the butter on top and sprinkle over the nutmeg. Cook in the oven for 40 minutes by which time a skin will have formed on the top. Serve immediately.

Notes

Reduce the amount of sugar if you find on your first try that the pudding is too sweet for you. Do not bother measuring the butter -guess the amount at about a dessert spoonful. This dessert is delicious enough on its own but if I wish to spoil myself I eat it with cream or ice cream.

Christmas Pudding

My daughter gave me a recipe which makes a superb Christmas pudding but it takes six hours to cook. Hanging around in a kitchen for that length of time does not appeal so I thought that I would get around to trying the recipe one day but never did. Then I found the recipe below which cuts the cooking time and gives a pudding almost as good. Making small puddings has two advantages - it reduces the cooking time to only an hour and any unwanted puddings can be stored in a freezer for use at a later date.

metric	*Ingredients*	*imperial*
150g	*self raising flour*	*5oz*
1tsp	*baking powder*	*1tsp*
1tsp	*mixed spice*	*1tsp*
50g	*butter*	*2oz*
2	*eggs*	*2*
1tbsp	*black treacle*	*1tbsp*
125ml	*stout*	*4floz*
411g jar	*sweet mincemeat*	*14oz jar*
1	*cooking or dessert apple*	*1*
175g	*currants*	*6oz*
1	*lemon*	*1*
1	*orange*	*1*
25g	*pecan nuts*	*1oz*

You will also need eight cup sized foil pudding basins and some greaseproof paper and aluminium foil. These can be bought at a supermarket.

Method

Do the tedious work first. Draw around a pudding basin so that you can cut out enough circles of greaseproof paper to fit the mouth of each basin. Next cut the same number of foil squares slightly bigger than the circles and put to one side. Preheat the oven to 180°C. Now rub the orange and lemon against the rough side of a grater to give zest - this is the name for scrapings of peel.

Measure together the flour, baking powder and spice and sieve into a large bowl. Add the eggs and then the butter which has been softened in a microwave or bowl of hot water. Mix thoroughly. Put the treacle into a glass bowl and soften as above so that it is easier to work then add the stout and stir until the treacle dissolves. Add the stout and treacle to the flour mixture and stir strongly using a large spoon or electric whisk. Finally chop the nuts and the apple and add together with the orange and lemon zest, currants, and mincemeat to the mixture and stir thoroughly.

Add a small amount of vegetable oil to each pudding dish and wipe out with a kitchen tissue - this prevents the pudding sticking to the basin. Divide the pudding mixture equally between the basins with a spoon. Melt a small amount of butter, extra to the recipe, in a dish. Cover each of the basins with one of the circles of greaseproof paper coated with the melted butter. Then cover each one with a square of foil squeezed tightly under the edge of the basin. Place the basins in a shallow roasting tray and pour in about 1cm ($1/2$ inch) of hot water. Cook in the oven for one hour. When slightly cooled the puddings should slide out of the basins but if not use a knife to carefully ease them out. Serve with cream, ice cream, custard or brandy butter.

Notes

You can drink the remaining stout and eat the bald orange as you wish. If you want to reheat the puddings put them in an oven or remove them from the foil basin before putting them in a microwave. If you wash the basins carefully you can use them again.

Cartoon Cook Book... for Men

Blackberry Batter Pudding

This dish is popular in Normandy where it is known as clafouti - a fruit pastry or thick pancake. You might think that I came across the recipe while dining in a charming little restaurant in France but the truth is much less interesting - I found it in a woman's magazine! I checked the recipe for authenticity in a well respected French cookery book where I found that milk was used instead of the butter and cream listed below. So if you are calorie and fat conscious try replacing half the cream by 100ml (4floz) of milk and 25g (1oz) of plain flour. Traditionally clafouti is made with black cherries but you can also try using raspberries, or apples and raisins.

metric	*Ingredients*	*imperial*
225g	*blackberries*	*8oz*
1tbsp	*cornflour*	*1tbsp*
1tsp	*ground cinnamon*	*1tsp*
1	*egg*	*1*
½ tsp	*vanilla essence*	*½ tsp*
25mg	*butter*	*1oz*
25mg	*plain flour*	*1oz*
100ml	*single cream*	*4floz*
50g	*caster sugar*	*2oz*
pinch	*baking powder*	*pinch*

Method

Preheat the oven to 200°C. Sieve the cornflour and cinnamon over the blackberries in a shallow one litre (1³/₄ pint) pie dish which has been lightly greased with vegetable oil. Try to cover the blackberries as as evenly as possible. Melt the butter in a dish in a microwave or by immersing in hot water. Place all the other ingredients with the melted butter in a large bowl and whisk to form a thick batter. Pour over the blackberries and bake for 40 minutes when the pudding will be brown and slightly risen. Sieve a fine layer of icing sugar over the pudding and serve with cream, ice cream or créme fraiche.

Notes

If you use cherries there is no need to toss them in the flour and cinnamon. The French use black cherries with the stones left in for extra flavour - not something I recommend, perhaps their teeth are stronger than ours!! I once made the mistake of not using a shallow pie dish and the pudding failed to cook right through - if you think in terms of a thick pancake you will not make the same mistake.

Whisky Rice Pudding

Rice pudding was very popular when I was a child and I remember clearly arguing with my sisters over who was to have the skin which formed on the top and was particularly delicious. Indeed it was so prized that if something happens which is of no importance to me I tend to say "it is no skin off my rice pudding". Today it is rarely listed in cookery books or offered in restaurants and I do not think that I have ever been served rice pudding at a dinner party. Perhaps it is thought that rice pudding is too ordinary - this version with its use of whisky, ginger marmalade and cream by no means satisfies this description so give it a try.

metric	*Ingredients*	*imperial*
200ml	single cream	7floz
50g	sugar	2oz
1tsp	vanilla essence	1tsp
2tbsp	ginger marmalade	2tbsp
25g	butter	1oz
4	eggs	4
2tbsp	whisky	2tbsp
100g	pudding rice	4oz
pinch	ground nutmeg	pinch

Method

Preheat the oven to 180°C. Place the rice in a large saucepan with the cream and 500ml (17floz) of hot water. Bring to the boil stirring continuously to prevent the cream from scorching then leave to simmer gently for 15 minutes. While waiting for the rice to cook melt the butter in a dish in a microwave or by immersing the dish in hot water. Separate the yolks from the whites of two of the eggs by breaking and allowing the white to run away by pouring the yolk from one half shell to the other shell. To the butter add the ginger marmalade, vanilla essence, sugar, eggs and egg yolks and then the whisky stirring between each addition to form a smooth mixture. Once the rice has cooked pour the contents of the saucepan into a 1 litre (1¾ pint) pie dish. Add the whisky mixture stirring so that the rice is evenly spread. Sprinkle over the nutmeg and cook in the oven for 40 minutes.

Notes

This rice pudding is delicious on its own but to really pig out eat it with cream. The two separated egg whites can be discarded or put in the fridge to use later. You can make the pudding without the whisky if you prefer or do not have any - unless you like whisky do not buy a large bottle just for this recipe - a miniature will do.

Exotic Bread and Butter Pudding

This is essentially an old recipe jazzed up by the introduction of more exotic ingredients such as bananas and glacé cherries. If you like the taste of apricots and figs these can be used instead of the bananas.

metric	*Ingredients*	*imperial*
6	bread slices	6
2	bananas small	2
50g	glacé cherries	2oz
2	eggs	2
2tbsp	seedless raisins or sultanas	2tbsp
300ml	milk	½ pint
1tbsp	sherry	1tbsp

A small amount of vegetable oil to grease the pie dish and sufficient butter and jam to coat the bread are also required.

Method

Lightly grease a one litre (1¾ pint) pie dish with the oil. Butter and jam the bread and cut each slice into four triangles. Chop the cherries into quarters. Line the bottom of the dish with eight triangles of bread, jam side up. Spread over one of the bananas sliced, one tablespoon of raisins and half the chopped cherries. Repeat another layer of bread and fruit retaining a few of the pieces of cherries and some of the raisins. Add the third layer of bread and sprinkle over the few remaining cherries and raisins to decorate the top of the pudding. Beat the eggs, the milk and the sherry with a fork and pour over the bread and fruit layers. Press down the bread with a fork so that it absorbs the egg and milk mixture and leave for 15 minutes. Switch on the oven to 190°C so that when the 15 minutes has elapsed it is should be up to temperature. Bake for 45 minutes when the top should be crisp and brown. Serve with cream or ice cream.

Notes

Depending on your taste brandy or rum can be used instead of the sherry. Also any jam can be used - I prefer pineapple or apricot.

Apple Crisp

The unusual combination of ground rice and desiccated coconut used to make the crust attracted me to this recipe. Apple crisp goes well with custard, cream or ice cream to make a dessert which is enjoyable but not quite up to the "I must have a second helping" class. Try it and see what you think. If you have a sweet tooth the recipe is about right for you - if not leave out the sugar when you stew the apples.

metric	Ingredients	imperial
3	dessert apples medium size	3
1tbsp	sugar	1tbsp
1tsp	baking powder	1tsp
25g	ground rice	1oz
50g	desiccated coconut	2oz
50g	margarine	2oz
50g	caster sugar	2oz
½ tsp	almond or vanilla essence	½ tsp
1	egg	1
2tbsp	jam	2tbsp

Method

Preheat the oven to 200°C. Peel, core and chop the apples and stew in boiling water in a saucepan for 15 minutes with one tablespoon of sugar. Put the margarine in a small bowl and melt by placing in a microwave or hot water for a minute or so. Mix the caster sugar into the margarine and stir in the almond or vanilla essence and the egg. Sieve into the mixture the baking powder and the ground rice then stir in the coconut until a thick paste is obtained. Grease a shallow one litre (1¾ pints) oven proof pie dish with a small amount of vegetable oil and after straining off the water spread the apples over the bottom. Dilute the jam with twice its volume of water and pour over the apples. Spread the coconut mixture evenly over the apples and bake in the oven for 20 minutes when the crust should be brown and firm.

Notes

The jam is added to give extra flavour so you can use any variety according to taste. My favourite is ginger marmalade as this gives a spicy flavour to the apples - sometimes I add a couple of tablespoons of currants or sultanas for extra zing. The ground rice can be bought at supermarkets but if I run short I grind my own using a clean coffee grinder.

Ginger Soufflé

While in my view one should cook for taste rather than show if a dish is both attractive to look at and tasty all to the good. This dish satisfies both criteria assuming you like the taste of ginger. Served with sweet syrup or cream it is delicious.

metric	*Ingredients*	*imperial*
25g	*butter*	*1oz*
25g	*self raising flour*	*1oz*
200ml	*milk*	*7floz*
4	*eggs*	*4*
25g	*crystallised ginger*	*1oz*
1tsp	*ground ginger*	*1tsp*

Method

Preheat the oven to 200°C. Grease the inside of a 18cm by 7cm (7 inch by 3 inch) pudding dish using a small amount of vegetable oil. Separate the eggs and place the whites in one dish and the yolks in another. Melt the butter in a large saucepan, stir in the flour and heat for a few minutes. Remove from the heat and add the milk slowly stirring well between each addition. Return the pan to the stove and bring to the boil slowly, stirring continuously until the sauce thickens. Remove the pan from the stove and beat in the egg yolks. Chop the crystallised ginger very finely and add to the pan with the ground ginger, stirring well. Whisk the whites in a large bowl using an electric whisk (or a fork) until removing the whisk leaves firm peaks which keep their shape. Carefully fold the whites into the mixture in the saucepan being careful not to over stir. Pour the mixture into the greased dish and cook for 30 minutes by which time the soufflé should have risen and its top should be golden brown.

Notes

Since soufflés can be tricky read the recipe for leek soufflé before trying this one. Whisking can be done with a fork but an electric whisk is so much easier.

Pancakes

Pancakes are usually associated with Pancake Day (Shrove Tuesday) when they are traditionally eaten in most British homes but they are so delicious that I often wonder why they are not served more frequently during the year. Why is it that pancakes are rarely served in restaurants in this country - they are not difficult to make and use readily available ingredients? In France (crêpes) and America there are restaurants dedicated to the sale of pancakes with a variety of fillings both sweet and savoury. The American way of eating plain pancakes with bacon, egg and sausage covered with maple syrup can be quite off-putting but having tried it I now rate it as one of my favourite breakfasts. This recipe is exactly as it was given to me by an American friend and you will see that it uses volume measures. Three tablespoons of melted butter equate to about twenty five grammes (one ounce) so judge this amount by cutting from a packet of known weight and melt it in a dish in a microwave or hot water. The pancakes can be eaten with lemon juice, maple syrup, cream or as I like it with ice cream. The fact that I like most desserts served with ice cream may come from my Italian grandfather who could not speak much English yet earned his living by making ice cream to sell from a handcart in the streets.

Ingredients

1¼ cups	plain flour
2 tbsp	sugar
2½ tsp	baking powder
¾ tsp	salt
1	egg
1¾ cups	milk
3 tbsp	melted butter

Method

Very lightly grease a non stick frying pan with olive or any other vegetable oil and put it on a low heat to warm up. Sift the flour, baking powder, salt and sugar into a bowl and mix together. Warm the milk slightly in a microwave or on the stove and add to the melted butter. Beat the egg, add to the milk and butter mixing well together before stirring into the flour mixture to give a cream like consistency. Raise the heat of the stove until a drop of water added to the frying pan begins to dance. Drop two tablespoons of the mixture into the pan which should spread to form a round about four inches in diameter. Cook until the top has dried then ease away the edges from the pan using a fish slice before turning over to cook the other side. Both sides should be a golden brown but if not keep turning until you get the desired result - lower the heat if the pancake starts to burn. This recipe makes six pancakes - if you want more or less you can adjust the size but larger pancakes are more difficult to handle.

Cartoon Cook Book... for Men   *Pancakes*

Notes

The traditional British way of making pancakes does not use butter and involves adding currants to the pancake as it cooks in the pan. Vary the recipe to suit yourself. If you use cold milk the melted butter will solidify and be more difficult to mix evenly into the flour mixture. You can if you like try tossing instead of using a fish slice to turn the pancakes and if you have lightly greased the pan as directed you will not splash oil over yourself. If you serve pancakes as a dessert they need to be eaten straight from the pan so make it easy on yourself by selecting a previously cooked or easily prepared main course.

"Fried Egg"

Banana and Coconut Fritters

A recent survey has suggested that bananas have become more popular than apples with the British public who it seems have been influenced by the sight of tennis players and other sportsman in play on television eating bananas as a quick source of energy. It appears that in terms of affecting public taste the apple a day to keep the doctor away cannot compete with the television image of bananas as a modern energy food. In the field of cooking however, there are very few recipes which use bananas compared to the many which use apples so this one, which I think is Indian in origin, is worth noting.

metric	*Ingredients*	*imperial*
100g	*plain flour*	*4oz*
2	*bananas*	*2*
1	*egg*	*1*
2tbsp	*desiccated coconut*	*2tbsp*
1tbsp	*milk*	*1tbsp*
1tbsp	*sugar*	*1tbsp*
½ tsp	*baking powder*	*½ tsp*
½ tsp	*vanilla essence*	*½ tsp*
1tsp	*vegetable oil*	*1tsp*
25g	*butter*	*1oz*

Method

Put the coconut in a bowl and add the milk, vanilla essence, beaten egg and sugar. Stir well. Then chop the bananas as small as possible and mash into the coconut mixture with a fork until smooth and virtually lump free. Sieve in the flour and baking powder and add enough water to give a thick batter which will just flow off the fork. Fry tablespoonfuls of the batter in the oil and butter until brown on both sides. Dust with sugar and serve with cream or ice cream. This recipe makes about eight fritters.

Notes

When vanilla is required most recipes will specify vanilla essence which is the natural extract from the vanilla pod. Vanilla flavouring is the artificial equivalent which costs about a third of the price. Either can be used in this recipe.

Tiramisu

I had never heard of tiramisu until I tasted it for the first time in a restaurant in London some years ago - now every Italian restaurant has it on the menu. The only time it has disappointed me was when I ordered tiramisu in a small ristorante on a holiday in Italy where I fully expected to find it at its best - it came prepacked in a small tub like ice cream. Tiramisu is particularly simple to make as it does not require cooking - it goes down well after a pasta main course and since it can be made the night before it is convenient to serve at a dinner party when the main course requires a lot of attention.

metric	*Ingredients*	*imperial*
250g	*mascarpone cheese*	*9oz*
2tbsp	*caster sugar*	*2tbsp*
2	*eggs*	*2*
125g	*sponge finger biscuits*	*5oz*
3tsp	*instant coffee*	*3tsp*
1tbsp	*brandy*	*1tbsp*
1tbsp	*cocoa*	*1tbsp*

Method

Dissolve the coffee in a mug of hot water and allow to cool in a small bowl. Separate the eggs by breaking against the side of a dish and allowing the whites to drain into a dish while pouring the yolks from one half eggshell to the other. Mix the cheese, sugar and egg yolks together with a fork. In another basin beat the egg whites until they form peaks when the whisk is lifted out and then fold into the cheese mixture. Add the brandy to the coffee then dip half of the sponge fingers in one at a time and place at the bottom of a one litre (1¾ pint) serving dish. Pour over half the cheese mixture. Repeat the process to form a second layer of sponge fingers and cheese. Sieve the cocoa over the top and leave to chill in a fridge for at least two hours before serving.

Notes

An electric whisk makes light work of aerating the egg whites but without one try a fork and a lot of effort. To fold the egg whites into the cheese mixture use a wide bladed knife and stir slowly so that as much air as possible is kept in the mixture - do not over stir. If you are worried about eating uncooked eggs replace them and the sugar with 200 grammes (7 ounces) of sweetened condensed milk. Instead of the brandy you can use whisky or sherry or indeed any spirits that blend well with the taste of coffee. Be quick when dipping the biscuits into the coffee as when soggy they can fall apart.

Home-made Ice Cream

I have seen numerous recipes for ice cream but almost all required either the use of special equipment or the mixture had to be put in the freezer and taken out at intervals to break up the ice crystals which formed. No such nonsense with this recipe - it is very simple and produces ice cream of the highest quality. I doubt if my Italian grandfather who sold ice cream for a living ever produced anything better than this. Just one criticism - for the diet conscious it does contain a lot of cream.

metric	**Ingredients**	*imperial*
2	eggs separated	2
50g	icing sugar	2oz
150ml	double cream	¼ pint
	Flavourings (your choice)	
2tsp	vanilla essence	2tsp
2tsp	coffee essence	2tsp
{ 2tsp	rum essence	2tsp }
{ 50g	and raisins	2oz }

Method

Select one of the three flavourings listed. Separate the eggs. Whisk the egg whites until very stiff and gradually whisk in the icing sugar. Whisk the egg yolks and the flavouring together then whisk into the egg whites. Lightly whisk the cream and gradually stir gently into the other ingredients with a large spoon. If you have decided to use the rum and raisins now add the raisins. Pour into a plastic container and place in a freezer overnight.

Notes

There are three different flavourings which produce three superb ice creams. The raisins in the rum and raisin recipe tend to fall to the bottom but no matter, none of my guests have complained - they are usually fighting over who gets second helpings. Finally you will note that this recipe uses uncooked eggs so the risk of salmonella must be mentioned. For me the ice cream is so delicious that the very small risk is worth taking but this is for you to decide.

Orange Creams

If you are looking for a dessert to impress your friends look no further. Imagine the surprise when you offer guests plain oranges which when opened are found to be filled with a delicious mousse. On the downside this recipe is a little fiddly to prepare though well worth the effort. It was given to me by a friend in Australia - whether it is his own idea I am not sure but I have never seen it anywhere else.

metric	*Ingredients*	*imperial*
4	*large oranges*	*4*
135g size	*orange jelly*	*4½ oz size*
300ml	*whipping cream*	*½ pint*
1tbsp	*lemon juice*	*1tbsp*
2tbsp	*sugar*	*2tbsp*

Method

Cut the top off each orange at the stalk end and scoop out the flesh using a spoon. Make sure you do not break the shell - if you do, any small holes can be plugged with edible materials such as softened bread. Scrape the flesh into a sieve and drain the juice into a basin - you can press the flesh with the back of a spoon or just simply squeeze with your fingers to get all the juice out. Make the juice up to 400ml (¾ pint) in a measuring jug with water, add the lemon juice and bring to the boil in a saucepan. Remove from the heat and add the jelly and sugar stirring well. Leave to cool then whisk in the cream. Pour the mixture into the shells and stand in a fridge until it sets - this usually takes a few hours.

Notes

Offer your guests the oranges on small plates to convey the impression that you are providing plain fruit for dessert. You can decorate the top of the mousse with cream or any topping of your choice. You can cool the juice quickly if you want by placing the container in iced water.

Lemon Syllabub

When we have American friends staying with us we almost always take them out for the evening to a medieval banquet at a local castle -there are three castles within ten miles of our house. A medieval feast is recreated in the dungeon or banqueting hall, a baron and baroness are selected from the guests to oversee the proceedings and with the wine flowing freely a good time is had by all. The entertainment consists of a meal followed by folk-singing which on its own is worth the price of admission. The meal usually consists of cawl (a stew of meat and vegetables), Welsh lamb and potatoes with a dessert of lemon syllabub. This old-fashioned sweet is rarely seen on restaurant menus which is a pity since it is delicious and easy to make. The recipe below makes four generous portions but can easily be used to serve six people.

metric	**Ingredients**	*imperial*
100g	*caster sugar*	*4oz*
2	*lemons*	*2*
600ml	*double cream*	*1 pint*
4tbsp	*sherry*	*4tbsp*

Method

Scrape the skin off the lemons - I use a cheese grater which gives me shreds of just the right size. Cut the lemons into pieces in a bowl, squeeze out the juice and sieve off the flesh. Put the juice, lemon shreds (known as zest) with the sugar and sherry in a bowl and whisk together. Next, whisk the cream until thick then slowly whisk in the lemon mixture. Pour into glasses and put in the fridge for a few hours before serving with good quality crisp biscuits such as brandy snaps.

Notes

This dessert is very useful from the time aspect since you can make it the night before a party to leave in the fridge overnight. You can use brandy or indeed any other spirit to suit your taste. As you will appreciate this dessert is loaded with calories but you can use cream substitutes if you prefer.

Simple Sherry Trifle

This recipe is simplicity itself - no cooking or preparation of the ingredients is required. It is a hearty dessert which is always very popular with adults and children (if you leave out the sherry) and is ideal for a buffet where people can dig in to help themselves. It is the type of dessert you would choose for guests who appreciate a good old-fashioned sweet.

metric	Ingredients	imperial
175g size	jam filled Swiss roll	6oz size
135g size	strawberry jelly	4½ oz size
415g	canned mixed fruit	14oz
425g	canned custard	14oz
300ml	whipping cream	½ pint
2tbsp	sherry	2tbsp

Method

Cut the Swiss roll into slices and place at the bottom of a 1½ litre (2½ pint) ornamental serving dish and pour over the sherry. Cut up the jelly and dissolve in about an half pint of hot water. Make up to a pint with the juice from the can of fruit and cold water. Pour over the Swiss roll in the dish and leave to set. Spread the fruit over the jelly and pour over the custard. Finally whip the cream and spread over the top of the custard. Leave in a fridge until needed.

Notes

If you are fat conscious use a cream substitute. The weights of the ingredients may seem odd for example 135 grammes of jelly - these just happen to be the packet and can sizes which are available in shops. The top of the trifle can be decorated with chopped almonds, chocolate flakes etc..

Pears in Wine

Some desserts for example a recipe for pears in red wine which I found in a book on Mediterranean cooking look much nicer than they taste. The deep red colour of the wine sauce set against the white of the cream with which it was served looked good on the plate but the taste did not pass my lip smacking "I want some more" test. Although not an advocate of pretty food I thought I would keep the recipe for an occasion when I needed a light dessert which looked nice on the table. Then a friend gave me the recipe below which makes a dessert which although not as attractive to the eye tastes much better.

metric	*Ingredients*	*imperial*
4	*large ripe pears*	*4*
25g	*butter*	*1oz*
150ml	*marsala wine*	*¼ pint*

Method

Peel the pears, cut into quarters and remove the cores. Melt the butter in a frying pan, add the pears and fry for a few minutes using a spoon to coat the pears with the butter. Add the marsala and heat slowly until the sauce begins to bubble and become tacky. Put the pears on warmed plates, spoon over the sauce and serve immediately with ice cream.

Notes

Any type of pear will do but the cooking time made need to be varied according to their ripeness. Marsala is a sweet fortified wine which originated in Sicily. The amount you use is not critical so you can slosh it into the pan in the manner of all good television chefs. The combination of hot pears and cold ice cream is delicious but perhaps not good enough to justify buying a bottle of Marsala if you do not like sweet dessert wine. You can try the recipe with port or sherry if that is what you have available in your drinks cabinet.

Cartoon Cook Book… for Men

IF I KNEW YOU WERE COMING ?

If I knew you were coming I would have baked a cake is a line from an old song and it is true that homemade cake with tea or coffee makes for a warm welcome. The ability to bake a cake gives one a certain self-satisfaction and family, friends and perhaps a special someone cannot fail to be impressed by your going to the trouble of making a cake for them. Try giving cakes you have made as presents for birthdays or at Christmas. For example, the mincemeat cake featured first was made by me for friends to celebrate with a bottle of whisky a hole in one achieved at my local golf course.

Some small points before we come to the recipes. Always follow the instructions carefully and do not be tempted to satisfy your curiosity by opening the oven door too soon otherwise your cake might get that sinking feeling. To test if a cake is cooked, at the specified time insert a knife into the centre - if it comes out clean the cake is ready. If you find the cake is not cooked but the top is beginning to burn, cover with aluminium foil and return it to the oven.

MENU - CAKES

Cakes **Page**

1. Mincemeat. 138
2. Tea. 139
3. Spiced Raisin and Apple. 140
4. Christmas. 141
5. Orange Carrot. 142
6. Ginger. 143
7. Eccles. 144
8. Spice. 146
9. Chocolate Coffee Sponge. 147
10. Hedgehog. 149

Mincemeat Cake

No, this cake does not contain meat but is made with mincemeat which is a mixture of currants, raisins, apples and suet. This was the first cake I ever baked so I would like to say that it is made with a traditional recipe handed down in my family from generation to generation but it would not be true - it was given to me by a friend. Like a lot of cooking, making a cake is not too difficult - all you need is to measure out the right amounts of the ingredients, mix well and cook for the correct time at the right temperature. This is the cake I made to celebrate a hole in one with friends at my local golf club. It went down very well but perhaps the whisky I supplied with it contributed something to the occasion!!

metric	*Ingredients*	*imperial*
400g	*sweet mincemeat*	*14oz*
75g	*mixed dried fruit*	*3oz*
225g	*self-raising flour*	*8oz*
2	*eggs*	*2*
150g	*sugar*	*5oz*
150g	*margarine*	*5oz*
50g	*glacé cherries*	*2oz*

Method

Preheat the oven to 170°C. Measure out all the ingredients. Chop the cherries into about four pieces each and the margarine into lumps so that it is easier to mix. Grease and line a 20cm (8 inch) round cake tin. Break the eggs into a large bowl removing any shell fragments if necessary. Add all the other ingredients and beat well until thoroughly mixed. Put the mixture into the cake tin, smoothing the surface with a wet knife. Bake in the middle of the oven for 2 hours by which time the cake should be golden brown and an inserted knife comes out clean. If not return to the oven .

Notes

To grease the inside of the cake tin use the margarine wrapper adding more margarine as necessary. To line the tin use greaseproof paper cut to size - the margarine will help the paper stay in place. I prefer the type of cake tin which has a loose bottom which can be pushed out to remove the cake.

Tea Cake

This is not the tea cake of the toasted variety which you eat with butter and jam but it is a cake that uses tea as an essential ingredient in the recipe. I say essential but quite frankly how it works and how the tea contributes to the cake is a mystery to me. It could also be called "help to get thin quick cake" as it contains no fat and so is worth noting by anyone wanting to lose weight. Indeed the recipe was given to me by my daughter but I believe it comes from a cook book for slimmers.

metric	**Ingredients**	*imperial*
450g	*mixed fruit*	*1lb*
2	*tea bags*	*2*
150g	*muscovado sugar*	*5oz*
225	*flour self raising*	*8oz*
1	*egg*	*1*

Method

The night before you want to make the cake pour 400ml (³/₄ pint) of boiling water over the tea bags in a medium sized bowl, stir and leave for 5 minutes. Remove the tea bags, add the mixed fruit to the tea and leave overnight covered with a plate or cloth. The next day preheat the oven to 180°C. Break the egg into a cup, beat and place in a large bowl. Add the sugar and mix together thoroughly with a large spoon. Sieve in the flour and stir again until completely mixed. Sieve the mixed fruit to remove most of the tea and then add to the bowl with the other ingredients and stir once more. Grease with margarine and line with greaseproof paper the inside of a 20cm (8 inch) round cake tin. Spoon the mixture into the tin smoothing and levelling the top with the back of a wet spoon or a knife. Bake at 180 C. for 1³/₄ hours in the centre of the oven by which time the cake should be dark brown and a knife inserted in it comes out clean.

Notes

This cake uses few ingredients and is very easy to make and if you are keen to cut down on your fat intake it is ideal for you.

Spiced Raisin and Apple Cake

I like spicy things so this recipe had immediate appeal and I was not disappointed with the cake it produced. When served hot it makes an excellent dessert but it is equally good as a cake with tea or coffee. I am very partial to any type of cake served with ice cream so this is my favourite way of eating spiced raisin and apple cake but it can be eaten also with cream or custard as you prefer.

metric	*Ingredients*	*imperial*
150g	margarine	*5oz*
2	eggs	*2*
225g	caster sugar	*8oz*
225g	self raising flour	*8oz*
1tsp	mixed spice	*1tsp*
2	medium to large dessert apples	*2*
100g	seedless raisins	*4oz*
1tbsp	demerara sugar	*1tbsp*

Method

Preheat the oven to 160°C. Lightly grease with a small amount of margarine the bottom and inside of a 20cm (8inch) round cake tin and line with greaseproof paper. Melt the margarine in a bowl in a microwave or by placing in hot water then stir in the eggs, caster sugar and mixed spice. Sieve in the flour and stir to form a thick dough. Place half of the dough in the cake tin and spread evenly using a wet knife. Peel, core and thinly slice one of the apples and place in the tin. Add the raisins and repeat with the second apple. Spread over the remaining dough as evenly as possible and sprinkle on the demerara sugar. Bake for $1^3/_4$ hours when the top should be brown and an inserted knife comes out clean.

Notes

When layering the apples and raisins try to keep them away from the sides of the tin and the centre. This prevents the cake from forming three layers and makes it easier to serve. Use a sharp knife to cut the cake otherwise with its firm crust and soft centre it can crumble.

Christmas Cake

When I first saw this recipe I was not impressed by its use of so much brandy - it seemed such a waste and expensive - nor by the fact that I would have to hang around in the house for three hours waiting for the cake to cook. It was just before Christmas so I tried it as a special treat using sherry instead of brandy and was very pleased with result. Certainly for a special occasion the quality of this cake justifies the expense, time and effort.

metric	**Ingredients**	*imperial*
8tbsp	brandy, port or sherry	8tbsp
1tsp	vanilla essence	1tsp
2tbsp	golden syrup	2tbsp
625g	mixed fruit	22oz
50g	glacé cherries	2oz
175g	dark brown sugar	6oz
175g	butter	6oz
225g	self raising flour	8oz
3	eggs	3

Method

Preheat the oven to 160°C. Melt the butter in a bowl in a microwave or by placing it in hot water. Pour the molten butter into a large saucepan, add two tablespoons of water and then all the other ingredients except the eggs and the flour. Bring to the boil gently and simmer for 5 minutes. Allow to cool for 20 minutes. In the meantime beat the eggs together in a bowl and mix in the flour until a smooth paste is obtained. When ready add the fruit mixture to the eggs and flour a little at a time stirring well. Line a 20cm (8 inch) cake tin with greaseproof paper and pour in the cake mixture. Bake for about three hours covering the top with greaseproof paper after one hour to prevent it burning. The cake is ready when a knife inserted in it comes out clean.

Notes

It can be difficult to measure out two tablespoons of the thick syrup so thin it by warming in a microwave for a minute or so. The mixed fruit is dried fruit which can be bought in a pack from a grocery store or supermarket. To accelerate the cooling the saucepan containing the fruit mixture can be placed in cold water. Lining the cake tin is done by cutting the greaseproof paper to size and sticking it to the bottom and sides of the tin using a small amount of butter or margarine.

Orange Carrot Cake

Carrot cake is usually found on sale in health food shops. I am not sure why this is so as I cannot believe this cake is more healthy to eat than many others but I do know it tastes good so it must do you good. Besides it is different to the more usual currant based cakes so it is worth adding to your repertoire.

metric	*Ingredients*	*imperial*
225g	*self raising flour*	*8oz*
100g	*margarine*	*4oz*
1	*orange*	*1*
1	*medium to large carrot*	*1*
1	*egg*	*1*
100g	*caster sugar*	*4oz*
2tbsp	*orange juice*	*2tbsp*
3tbsp	*milk*	*3tbsp*

Method

Preheat the oven to 180°C. Peel and grate the carrot. Grate the skin of the orange by rubbing the whole orange against the grater - you need about two heaped tablespoons of orange and four of carrot. Melt the margarine in a bowl by placing it in hot water or a microwave for a minute or so. Add the sugar, egg, orange juice, milk, grated orange peel and carrot and mix well with a fork. Sieve in the flour and beat well to form a thick dough. Grease the inside and bottom of a 20cm (8 inch) cake tin and line with greaseproof paper. Place the mixture in the tin and level as well as you can with a wet knife. Bake for 45 minutes by which time the top should be brown and a knife inserted into the cake comes out clean.

Notes

Squeeze the orange to obtain the two tablespoons of juice required. Place the cake in the oven on a grid not on a tray as it cooks more thoroughly when the air can circulate around the bottom.

Ginger Cake

I am very fond of the taste of ginger so when I was given a recipe for a Dutch ginger cake by a relative in Australia I was keen to try it. The recipe did give a good result but the cake was a little too rich for my taste which perhaps should have been expected because it contained 225g (8oz) of butter. The recipe below is a useful compromise - it is not too rich and has the right amount of gingery taste.

metric	*Ingredients*	*imperial*
100g	*margarine*	*4oz*
100g	*soft brown sugar*	*4oz*
2tbsp	*syrup*	*2tbsp*
50g	*crystallised ginger*	*2oz*
100ml	*milk*	*5floz*
1tsp	*bicarbonate of soda*	*1tsp*
175g	*self-raising flour*	*6oz*
1tsp	*ground ginger*	*1tsp*
1	*egg*	*1*

Method

Preheat the oven to 180°C. and measure out the margarine, sugar, and flour. Melt the margarine in a glass bowl in a microwave for a minute or so or by putting the bowl in an oven or hot water. Mix in the sugar, syrup, and milk and then stir in the bicarbonate of soda. Slowly sift the flour and ground ginger into the bowl and stir until smooth. Break the egg into a separate dish and beat before adding to the cake mixture. Mix thoroughly. Finally chop the crystallised ginger into small pieces and add to the bowl. Line a one litre (two pint) cake tin by rubbing the inside with margarine and then covering with greaseproof paper. Spoon the mixture into the cake tin and bake in the oven for 45 minutes by which time a knife inserted into the cake should come out clean.

Notes

Any syrup will do - maple, corn or golden. Turn out the cake on to a wire rack or plate and allow to cool before removing the greaseproof paper.

Eccles Cake

When I was a boy, my mother's fruit cake was much enjoyed by the family but as a special treat we would be taken to one of the bakeries which in those days seemed to be on every street corner to choose a cake for tea. Among the éclairs, ice slices, chelsea buns and custard tarts, top of my list came eccles cakes. Crammed with currants and still warm they were delicious. Therefore you will appreciate how much the recipe below attracted my attention when I first saw it. In its original form the recipe described how to make a number of small shop like cakes similar to the ones I bought as a child but to make it easy on myself I decided to make one big cake which I could cut it into slices.

metric	Ingredients	imperial
250g	frozen puff pastry	9oz
100g	currants	4oz
25g	chopped peel	1oz
50g	muscovado sugar	2oz
15g	butter	½ oz
1	lemon	1
½ tsp	ground nutmeg	½ tsp
½ tsp	allspice	½ tsp
½ tsp	ground ginger	½ tsp

Method

Preheat the oven to 220°C. Allow the pastry to defrost for a few hours before using. Melt the butter in a bowl in a microwave or by placing it in hot water. Add the sugar and stir until you have a smooth paste. Grate half the skin off the lemon - cut the lemon and squeeze out two teaspoons of juice and add with the skin and all the other ingredients to the bowl. Mix well. Roll out the pastry on a pastry board or clean work top until it is approximately 30cm by 20cm (12 by 8 inches). Trim the edges using the rolling pin as a straight rule to form a rectangle. Spread the currant mixture over the pastry evenly leaving about 3cm (1 inch) clear at one of the shorter sides. Brush this end with milk and carefully roll up the pastry towards it so that you have a roll. If some of the currant mixture falls out push it back in with your fingers and after brushing with milk squeeze the ends together as though you were packing a parcel. Brush the roll with milk and plunge a fork in a few times so that it can breathe. Sprinkle some caster sugar over the top. Grease a suitably sized baking tray with a small amount of vegetable oil on a piece of kitchen paper and place the roll on it with the join underneath. Bake for 20 minutes by which time it should have browned.

Notes

The mixed peel can be bought at shops or supermarkets. The roll when cold can be cut into slices and eaten as a cake but it is best served as a dessert with cream or ice cream.

Cartoon Cook Book... for Men *Eccles Cake*

Do not try measuring the butter guess it as about a dessert spoonful.

If you are keen to make individual cakes roll out the pastry to form a square about 25cm by 25cm (10 by 10 inches). Cut into four squares and place a quarter of the fruit mixture in the centre of each. Brush the edges of each of the squares with milk then pull up and squeeze together to form little bags enclosing the mixture completely. Turn over and press down to form flat round cakes. Make two small cuts in the top of each cake, brush with milk, sprinkle over caster sugar and bake as before.

"Poached Egg"

Spice Cake

This is my version of a cake recipe which I understand is over one hundred years old. It is not my favourite - in fact I did not particularly like the cake until I tried eating a slice with butter and cheese. This combination works well so it is certainly worth trying but remember it is different so do not be disappointed if it is not quite to your taste.

metric	Ingredients	imperial
450g	plain flour	1lb
350g	black treacle	12oz
50g	margarine	2oz
150ml	stout	¼ pint
50g	brown sugar	2oz
50g	candied peel	2oz
50g	sultanas	2oz
2tsp	ground ginger	2tsp
2tsp	ground coriander	2tsp
1tsp	bicarbonate of soda	1tsp

Method

Preheat the oven to 180°C. Linc a cake or loaf tin about 23 by 12cm (9 inch by 5inch) using greaseproof paper coated with a little butter or margarine to help it stick to the tin. Sieve the flour, ginger, coriander and bicarbonate of soda into a large bowl. Mix in the sugar, sultanas and candied peel. Put the treacle and the margarine in a saucepan, gently warm and mix together - add the stout slowly. If the stout is cold the margarine may solidify out so if it does stir it back in. Now pour the stout mixture into the bowl with all the other ingredients and stir well. Pour the mixture into the cake tin and bake for one hour by which time a knife inserted into the cake will come out clean.

Notes

If your treacle like mine comes in a tin remember you cannot warm it in a microwave oven to make it easier to pour. The cake will keep for sometime but if you like you can cut it into portions and store it in a freezer until required.

Chocolate Coffee Sponge Cake

Coffee is one of my favourite flavours and like most people I love chocolate so this recipe has instant appeal - it was given to me by a close friend but it was some years before I got around to trying it as I mislaid the paper it was written on. When I did try it I was not disappointed as the sponge was much to my liking. Mind, when I made it the first time it was a disaster - no fault of the recipe - a simple mistake on my part. I asked my wife to take the sponges out of the oven and leave them to cool on a wire rack. Later I coated them with the chocolate sauce without removing the lining paper - the coffee/paper/chocolate/ layer sponge cake was not a success!! The next time I tried it everything worked well and the result was well worth the effort. Below there are two chocolate sauces, the first is solid at room temperature and is used to coat the cake and the second which stays liquid can be poured over the cake hot or cold if you are the type that welcomes "death by chocolate".

metric	*Ingredients*	*imperial*
175g	*margarine*	*6oz*
175g	*self raising flour*	*6oz*
175g	*caster sugar*	*6oz*
3	*eggs*	*3*
2tsp	*instant coffee*	*2tsp*
200g	*plain chocolate*	*7oz*
25g	*butter*	*1oz*
2tbsp	*milk*	*2tbsp*
200g	*plain chocolate*	*7oz*
50g	*caster sugar*	*2oz*
100ml	*double cream*	*3½ floz*

Method

Preheat the oven to 180°C. Dissolve the coffee in one tablespoon of boiling water and allow to cool. Cut the margarine into small chunks so that it mixes easily, then mix with the coffee and all the other ingredients in a bowl - this is best done with an electric whisk but you can do it by hand. Line the bottoms of two shallow 18cm (7 inch) sponge tins with greaseproof paper and grease the sides with butter or vegetable oil and divide the cake mixture equally between them. Use a wet knife to spread the mixture evenly. Cook in the oven for 25-30 minutes by which time an inserted knife should come out clean.

To make the first chocolate sauce, break the chocolate into pieces and put with the milk and butter in a saucepan and warm very slowly stirring until smooth. Alternatively you can heat the mixture in a glass basin in a microwave. While the sauce is warm coat the top of both sponges and bring together so that you have layers of chocolate/sponge/

Chocolate Coffee Sponge Cake   Cartoon Cook Book... for Men

chocolate/sponge. The cake is now ready to eat but is best left until the chocolate has set. Ignore the second sauce unless you like to drown in chocolate. To make it break the chocolate into pieces and place in a saucepan with the caster sugar and 350 ml (13 floz) of water. Bring to the boil with constant stirring and simmer for a few minutes until the mixture is smooth. Allow to cool then stir in the cream. You now have a sauce which you can use poured around a slice as extra chocolate and a form of decoration when you serve the cake as a dessert.

Notes

The second chocolate sauce can be used to pour over ice cream and served as a dessert on its own. If you like a stronger taste of coffee you can use two teaspoons of instant coffee dissolved in two tablespoons of water instead of the milk in the sauce which is used to coat the sponge.

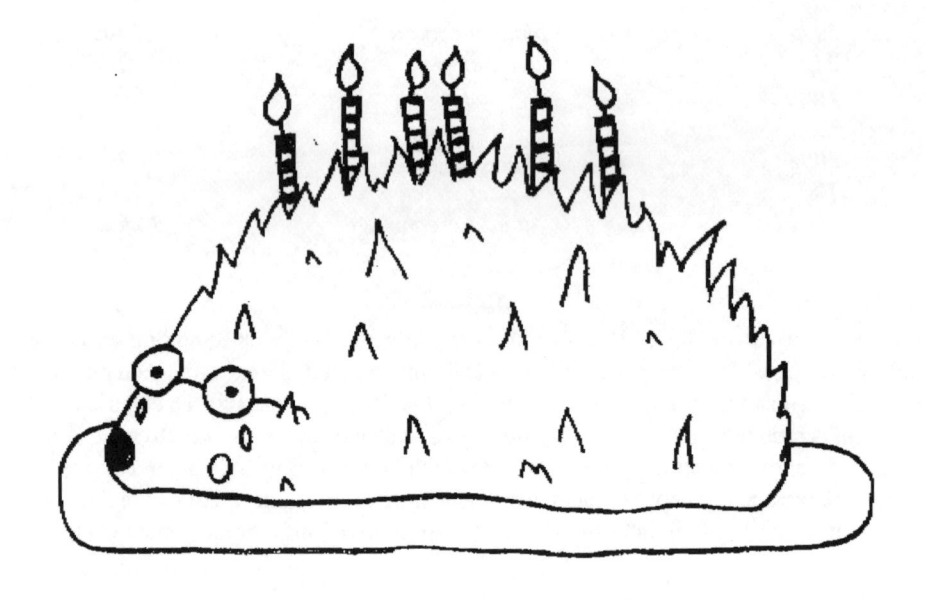

"Hedgehog Cake"

Hedgehog Cake

When hedgehog crisps were introduced as a sales gimmick sometime ago animal lovers became concerned so I had better record at the outset that this recipe has not been tested on hedgehogs nor does it contain anything derived from or connected with hedgehogs. The name comes about because the original recipe prescribed that the cake mixture be moulded and decorated to look like a hedgehog. When made this way the cake appeals to children who are intrigued by the shape but it can be made up in a more conventional form. This recipe also has the virtue that it is virtually non cook but on the other hand it is chock-a-block with calories so the weight conscious should beware.

metric	Ingredients	imperial
350g	digestive biscuits	12oz
200g	butter	7oz
75g	caster sugar	3oz
75g	crisp rice cereal	3oz
175g	raisins	6oz
5tbsp	cocoa	5tbsp
5tbsp	golden syrup	5tbsp
jar	chocolate spread	jar

Method

Crumb the biscuits in a large bowl or by using a blender. Add the rice cereal and the raisins and mix together. Melt the butter in a saucepan on a stove or in a bowl in a microwave, mix in the syrup, sugar and cocoa until smooth then finally stir in the biscuit mixture until combined thoroughly. Now comes the clever part if you feel up to it - turn the cake mixture on to a tray and mould with your hands to the shape of a hedgehog. At this stage I usually forget about hedgehogs and use a 20 centimetre (8 inch) cake tin with a push up bottom lined with greaseproof paper into which I pack the cake mixture and press down firmly. The cake is then left in a fridge for a few hours to set and finally the chocolate spread is used to coat the top and sides to give that finished look. If you have been bold and now have the hedgehog shape you must use your artistic ability to enhance its appearance using currants for eyes and so on.

Notes

Chocolate spread can be bought at stores and supermarkets - it is used as a spread in sandwiches. You will need to buy a jar but the size depends on the amount you use to decorate the cake. Another way to crumb the biscuits is to squeeze them together in a plastic bag.

Cartoon Cook Book... for Men

"A little wine adds interest to a stew"

Cartoon Cook Book... for Men

SAY CHEESE - AND WINE ??

To produce a smile you are often invited to say cheese - if you say cheese and wine it should guarantee a smile as one of the best ways of creating that "feeling good" feeling is to accompany a meal with a wine that you enjoy. Unfortunately there is an artificial mystique about wine which bewilders most men and leads them to judge the quality of a wine by its price. How many of us when asked by a waiter to taste the wine before serving have the confidence to turn it away if it does not taste quite right? How many of us have the aplomb to direct a waiter to pour the wine with a few words to the effect that we have every confidence in the ability of the restaurant to serve wine in the right condition. The answers to the questions I would suggest are very few of us - we would be too self conscious.

When asked to taste wine we are advised by experts to fill the glass about a third full so that we can swill it around to release the bouquet at the top of the glass. Then we are told to plunge the nose into the glass and breathe deeply before taking a sip to swirl around the mouth. Next we purse the lips and suck air over the top of the wine so that the aroma hits the back of the throat. And what does this achieve? One well known wine expert tells us that a sauvignon blanc should evoke scents of gooseberries and cat's pee; the gamay grape the smell of cherries, rubber and tar and the pinot noir the aroma of strawberries and compost heaps!! Coupled with this we are told that there is a right kind of wine for every course - shellfish require crisp acidic wines such as muscadet; delicate fish calls for a delicate wine like a riesling, whereas stronger tasting fish can tolerate fuller wines or even reds; beef, lamb and poultry go with burgundy and claret but pork should be served with a light red or fruity white wine; creamy cheeses go well with claret or beaujolais while heavier cheeses like stilton demand a heavier wine like port. What nonsense!!

My advice is to serve wines that you and your guests enjoy regardless of their price and pedigree. You do not drink a particular brand of beer because others tell you it is good, you drink it because you like it - why act differently with wines? Sweet wines such as lambrusco and liebfraumilch, although looked down on by so called connoisseurs of good wine are very popular and quite rightly so. Find reasonably priced wines which you like at your local store or supermarket and never be tempted to serve wines such as champagne as a special treat just because you are told they are "the best". On holidays abroad take the opportunity to experiment, try the local wines and make a note of the names of those you like so that you can seek them out when you return home. On one occasion I was served on a plane travelling abroad a small bottle of French white wine which tasted extra special. It took me some time to track it down at a local wine store but since then it has occupied pride of place on my dining table no matter what I am eating. One small reservation I have about this "drink what you like when you like" policy, I do not understand how wine can be appreciated with highly spiced Indian or Chinese meals. As an aperitif before the meal yes but otherwise??

There is very little I wish to say about cheese except that with good bread or biscuits it provides a good ending to a meal provided that you have not overindulged on the other courses. Eating cheese in France is a particular pleasure as even the smallest cafe provides a lavish cheese board which enables you to eat as much or as little as you want of what you want. French cheeses such as Brie, Camembert and Boursin, and the British cheeses Stilton and Caerphilly are much to my liking but if you prefer Cheddar enjoy it.

Printed in Great Britain
by Amazon.co.uk, Ltd.,
Marston Gate.